Risk Management for Software Projects

Titles in the IBM McGraw-Hill Series

Open Systems and IBM: Integration and Convergence
Pamela Gray   ISBN 0-07-707750-4

OS/2 Presentation Manager Programming: Hints and Tips
Bryan Goodyer   ISBN 0-07-707776-8

The IBM RISC System/6000
Clive Harris   ISBN 0-07-707668-0

The IBM RISC System/6000 User Guide
Mike Leaver and Hardev Sanghera   ISBN 0-07-707687-7

PC User's Guide: Simple Steps to Powerful Personal Computing
Peter Turner   ISBN 0-07-707421-1

Dynamic Factory Automation: Creating Flexible Systems for
Competitive Manufacturing
Alastair Ross   ISBN 0-07-707440-8

MVS Systems Programming
Dave Elder-Vass   ISBN 0-07-707767-9

The New Organization: Growing the Culture of Organizational
Networking
Colin Hastings   ISBN 0-07-707784-9

Commonsense Computer Security 2nd Edition: Your Practical
Guide to Information Protection
Martin Smith   ISBN 0-07-707805-5

CICS Concepts and Uses: A Management Guide
Jim Geraghty   ISBN 0-07-707751-2

Risk Management for Software Projects
Alex Down, Michael Coleman and Peter Absolon ISBN 0-07-707816-0

Investing in Information Technology: Managing the decision-making
process
Geoff Hogbin and David Thomas   ISBN 0-07-707957-1

The Advanced Programmer's Guide to AIX 3.x
Phil Colledge   ISBN 0-07-707663-X

The CICS Programmer's Guide to FEPI
Robert Harris   ISBN 0-07-707793-8

Details of these titles in the series are available from:

The Product Manager, Professional Books
McGraw-Hill Book Company Europe
Shoppenhangers Road, Maidenhead, Berkshire, SL6 2QL
Telephone: 0628 23432 Fax: 0628 770224

Alex Down, Michael Coleman, Peter Absolon

Risk Management for Software Projects

McGRAW-HILL BOOK COMPANY

London · New York · St Louis · San Francisco · Auckland
Bogotá · Caracas · Lisbon · Madrid · Mexico · Milan
Montreal · New Delhi · Panama · Paris · San Juan · São Paulo
Singapore · Sydney · Tokyo · Toronto

Published by
McGRAW-HILL Book Company Europe
Shoppenhangers Road, Maidenhead, Berkshire, SL6 2QL, England
Tel 0628 23432; Fax 0628 770224

British Library Cataloguing-in-Publication Data

Down, Alex
    Risk Management for Software Projects.—
(IBM McGraw-Hill Series)
    I. Title   II. Series
    005.1068

ISBN 0-07-707816-0

Library of Congress Cataloging-in-Publication Data

Down, Alex
    Risk management for software projects / Alex Down, Michael
Coleman, Peter Absolon.
        p. cm.—(IBM McGraw-Hill Series)
    Includes bibliographical references and index.
    ISBN 0-07-707816-0
    1. Computer software—Development. 2. Risk management.
I. Coleman, A. Michael. II. Absolon, Peter. III. Title.
IV. Series
QA76.D47D69 1994
005—dc20   93-28798
                                                                CIP

1234 CUP 9654

Typeset by Paston Press Ltd, Loddon, Norfolk
and printed and bound in Great Britain at the University Press, Cambridge

For my two children: Tom, who illustrated all the risks attendant on just one person working on a home computer project, and Emily, who is herself a formidable risk.
A.D.

For all who worked in the Product Assurance Laboratory at Hursley and learned the lesson of Matthew 13:57!
M.C.

For those who develop software at Hursley, and think none of this could happen to them. Well, it probably did!
P.A.

Contents

Foreword

The IBM McGraw-Hill Series

IBM UK and McGraw-Hill Europe have worked together to publish this series of books about information technology and its use in business, industry and the public sector.

The series provides an up-to-date and authoritative insight into the wide range of products and services available, and offers strategic business advice. Some of the books have a technical bias, others are written from a broader business perspective. What they have in common is that their authors—some from IBM, some independent consultants—are experts in their field.

Apart from assisting where possible with the accuracy of the writing, IBM UK has not sought to inhibit the editorial freedom of the series, and therefore the views expressed in the books are those of the authors, and not necessarily those of IBM.

Where IBM has lent its expertise is in assisting McGraw-Hill to identify potential titles whose publication would help advance knowledge and increase awareness of computing topics. Hopefully these titles will also serve to widen the debate about the important information technology issues of today and of the future—such as open systems, networking and the use of technology to give companies a competitive edge in their market.

IBM UK is pleased to be associated with McGraw-Hill in this series.

Sir Anthony Cleaver
Chairman
IBM United Kingdom Limited

Preface

Why should you need to read—let alone, buy—a book on risk management? After all, isn't the management of risk a life skill—something that comes naturally? For example, most of us drive. We all, at some time, overtake vehicles. In so doing we assess and evaluate many kinds of risks. We then act on our judgement and, 999 times out of 1000 (or thereabouts), that judgement is vindicated. When we are about to commit our lives—or, at the very least, the integrity of an expensive piece of machinery—on the basis of our risk judgement, we do so with awesome skill and enviable confidence. So why then, if good risk management is second nature to us, do so many software projects end up on the rocks?

The answer, in our view, is that when it comes to managing software projects, we so often fail to carry over our everyday risk management abilities. All of a sudden we find that:

- We never have enough time.
- Our resources always seem to be deficient.
- We do not have the information we need.
- People, for some reason, never seem to behave the way we want them to.
- Our environment becomes completely uncontrollable.

In other words, we become poor risk managers—and that is why you might find this book worth reading!

The book focuses on the reasons for poor risk management within software development and covers a number of practical methods for resolving the problems encountered. In particular, it focuses on a key concept: that of the optimum risk environment (ORE). Risk brings with it the opportunity both for failure and for success. In our simple overtaking analogy, even the least chancy manoeuvre is not totally without risk (the overtaken driver might take umbrage and speed up, for instance). As drivers, we determine for ourselves our own optimum risk level. So it is with software development: by working within an optimum risk framework, we set the boundaries for risks we are prepared to take.

There are four parts to the book:

1   Introduction—what risk means in terms of software development; the core considerations in dealing with risk; plans and processes.
2   Creating the optimum risk environment—anticipating risk and planning to deal with it; setting optimum risk levels through requirements and objectives specifications.
3   Managing within the optimum risk environment—risk in development; risk in verification; risk in product delivery.
4   Learning from the optimum risk environment—post-ship reviews; doing it better next time.

In addition, a number of appendices give essential processes and templates in a form that can be adapted to your situation.

The authors are all staff members at the IBM UK Laboratories, Hursley. Many of the techniques described herein have been tried, tested, refined, and tried again during the development of many of the most successful of Hursley's software products. That is why, in some measure, it would only be completely correct if every single member of the laboratory were credited here for their contribution towards this book. As that is not possible, we trust that those not named will accept our gratitude, and regard the following list as representative of those who have helped this particular development: Paul Gibson, Jeff Burwood, Peter Swithinbank, Norman Adlam, John Barfield, Steven Holmes, Keith Watson, Colin Daniels, Dick Allen, John Allan, Kathy Ferguson, Dave Coakley, Martin West, and Keith Taylor.

We also gratefully acknowledge the considerable help given by members of the IBM/McGraw-Hill series editorial team: Stephen Lockey, Jenny Ertle, Ros Comer, and Rupert Knight.

Alex Down, Michael Coleman, Peter Absolon
IBM UK Laboratories, Hursley

Part One
Risk basics

A linking thread running through this book is *thinking*, especially the right kind of thinking at the right time. Creative thinking, logical thinking, analytical and critical thinking all have their part to play in risk management. Some experienced risk-managers develop patterns of thinking within which they can exploit these qualities of thought. These managers are the successful ones, but their patterns, or paradigms, are often not recognized (even by themselves) because their thought patterns have evolved subconsciously and are difficult to pass on as experience to their followers.

In this part of the book, we have tried to distil the important patterns of thinking from what we have observed in successful risk managers. We have identified three basic patterns:

- An understanding of the way that *process* can be used to control risk.
- A questioning approach embodied in the building of good plans.
- A desire to quantify—to ascribe numbers to interesting characteristics—in order to control.

Note that these basic patterns are presented in a logical order; each depends on a foundation laid by the preceding one. Thus, a good plan can only be assured if an appropriate process is in place, and quantification is only really of use within the context of a good plan.

These patterns are described in the Chapters 2 and 3. We think that even experienced risk managers will find something of value in them.

One last point about the qualities of thinking required. They are almost never found in equal measure in one individual. If you are aware that you are better at, say, logical thinking than creative thinking, then acquire the services (if only on an ad hoc basis) of a friend or colleague who has the qualities in which you are weaker. You will learn from each other, and you will probably find that two (or three) heads are much better than one.

1
Running risks

1.1   The software risk dilemma

We are all good risk managers. The human race owes its survival to the fact that we can learn to spot risks, assess the dangers and work out strategies to avert them. The risks we run today may be less physical than those faced by our hunter–gatherer ancestors, but they are none the less real for that. It is not too fanciful to suggest that the skills honed by thousands of years of evolution to protect the hunter when pursuing wild animals are exactly the same as those we use when overtaking another car (or avoiding one coming in the other direction), and are exactly the same as those needed by a project manager to ensure, for example, that a test plan completes on schedule.

Why then do so many software projects end on the rocks? After all, there is not so great a difference between committing to an overtaking manoeuvre, and committing to a completion date:

- They both have to be done within a certain time (estimating).
- They both have to be done with what is available to you (resources).
- They both depend on people around you behaving in a reasonable way (dependencies).
- The circumstances in which you operate affect the way in which the job is done (environment).

We overtake with no trouble, so why is project completion a problem? In our view it is *poor risk management*. Risk management is crucial, but most of us do not manage to carry over our everyday abilities to the more demanding software arena.

Software development is done in a business world where risk is usually inherent in the business decisions that are made. Business decisions are often very difficult. The situation is often characterized by:

- Richness and complexity
- Qualitative information
- Subjective opinions

However, business people have tools for handling these decisions, and can usually resolve the decision into a choice between options, with the decision being made on expected-profit calculations. Risks are taken into account in the calculations through aggregation of probabilities and costs. Once the decision is made, it can usually be followed by concrete action that can be planned confidently.

In software development, on the other hand, the initial decision may be made to proceed with relatively little pain. An opportunity is identified, a solution sketched out, costs and benefits calculated, and a business case established. It is then that the real difficulties start. There is nothing concrete about an information system. In fact, most of the problems of developing software stem from its ephemeral nature—you cannot see it, you cannot touch it. Even designs are logical representations, and do not translate to anything that the ultimate user can relate to in the real world. Because you cannot touch it, it is difficult to measure, so you do not know how complete it is, or how good it is. It is therefore hard to answer questions like:

- Is it finished?
- Will it be finished on time?
- Is it going to be acceptable?
- Will the users like it?
- Will it work?
- How many problems will we hit later on?

However, by at least recognizing that there are questions that are hard to answer, we have taken the first step towards *analysing* risks.

The rest of this chapter clarifies the characteristics of risk and introduces a framework for the analysis of risk that is used throughout the book.

1.2   The characteristics of risk

We all drive, or sit critically beside someone else who drives, so we are all used to assessing the risks in an overtaking manoeuvre. That such a tiny proportion actually go wrong (in spite of the occasions when knuckles turn white, and hearts beat faster) is testimony to the fact that we can manage risk and cope supremely well when under threat. The accelerated heart beat is a natural reaction to a threat—the possibility of something undesirable happening. We only view circumstances as a threat if we are not sure of our own ability to control those circumstances, either because we will be operating at the limit of our performance, or because we are not sure what all the factors are. In other words, circumstances prompting risk are:

- Working at operational limits
- Uncertainty, unknowns

So a risk, in everyday life, is a set of circumstances that makes us nervous, because we perceive the possibility of an undesirable outcome. When 'possibility' becomes 'probability', then 'a risk' becomes 'a high risk' and makes us feel very uncomfortable indeed. (There is also of course the situation where we do not know that we do not know. We stay in ignorance until we are hit out of the blue by the unexpected. This is an undesirable outcome, but not a risk because there was no anticipation of it. More of this later.)

Our degree of nervousness is coloured by our *perception* of two things: the likelihood of an undesirable outcome (the mathematical probability), and exactly how undesirable the outcome appears. Thus the factors affecting perception of risk are:

- Probability of mishap
- Penalty associated with mishap

Both of these factors must have appreciable values before most people start to worry about risk, but even then our degree of nervousness can be overridden to some extent by perceived advantages accruing from a successful outcome. If overtaking means the difference between meeting an important client on time and failing to close the deal, then the perceived risk is compensated for by the perceived reward. Risk will only be accepted when it is compensated for by reward, though different people will have different ideas on the degree of compensation they need. Increased risk means that a greater reward will be required.

Where the risk circumstance is 'unknowns' then the obvious strategy is to collect the information needed to control the risk. This is rarely easy or cheap, and so it needs to be put in the context of the likely scale of penalties and rewards—the cost of controlling the risk considered against the possible loss incurred from the risk maturing, and the gain from avoiding the risk.

Similarly, where the circumstance is 'limits of performance', a strategy will be to provide support so that performance is extended beyond the point where the limit is a problem. Again, this is unlikely to be cheap, so an understanding of the likely reward relative to the penalty will help the risk manager.

Remember that reducing risk will almost inevitably cost money. It is relatively easy to reduce risk—the difficult bit is to keep the risk reduction commensurate with the benefits gained—but the products that get the balance right are the ones that are popular with their users, or succeed against their competitors.

Exactly when does a risk really begin to mean something? A risk itself is a potential for trouble. Almost always, when a risk matures, when a risk is realized, a commitment has not been met. The driver accelerating to overtake and the project manager signing a contract with a third-party developer both make commitments in their own way. When the overtaking driver is past the point when he can safely duck back in, or when the manager blots the ink dry on his signature, the commitment has been made, and both will have an expectation that the transaction that they have embarked on will have a satisfactory outcome, but if something goes wrong, they have real problems on their hands. So it is at the point of commitment that a risk really begins to mean something. Before then, we can afford to look dispassionately at the chances of success, weigh things up, and retain the right (usually) to withdraw gracefully if we do not fancy our chances.

It takes time and practice to develop our expectations for the outcomes of different situations. All drivers increase their skill in overtaking, from their first nervous trips out by themselves (when the judgements they make will probably be anything but quick and skilful) through to the advanced motorist stage. There are plenty of opportunities to practice, and when they do make a mistake, they can usually sink back into the anonymity of their seats, making a mental note never to do *that* again. In this case, learning is rapid, with direct and immediate feedback on the mistakes that are made. The very simple mental model that novices start out with quickly becomes more sophisticated, as they build up that degree of advanced self-protection known as roadcraft. Unfortunately, project managers do not have this advantage. Learning is usually very slow: it is difficult to relate the lessons to the decisions that precipitated them, because of the timescales involved. The store of experience that is the project management equivalent of roadcraft is slow and difficult to build up. Mistakes, which are necessary to learn, are sometimes 'rewarded' with swift removal from the management arena, thus ensuring that the same mistakes are doomed to be repeated by successors.

We all construct models in our minds to help us cope with the complexities of everyday life: we have expectations of how the car will accelerate in given circumstances, how to set the hot and cold taps to give the water temperature we like, and so on. These models evolve quickly, and we spend all our formative years developing this model-building facility which serves us well for most of our human undertakings—until we get to manage software projects. Suddenly, our models are found wanting. It takes many projects to develop the range of experience that can be built up relatively quickly on the road, and even experienced project managers will find that there are gaps in their ability to identify and handle project risks. This book cannot supply a complete set of models, but it can provide a good starter set, and a framework within which to build a comprehensive set.

1.3   The analysis of risk

1.3.1   Analysing risk

It needs creative thought as well as in-depth experience (models) both to identify and to control risks without spending so much that the financial viability of a project is destroyed. This sounds daunting even for experienced project managers, but we all have access to experience accumulated during our information technology (IT) careers, and this book provides supplementary experience (models) plus a framework to fit it all into. The basic framework is introduced here, with a familiar example.

Table 1.1 shows some of the factors that drivers take into account when

Table 1.1. Risks in overtaking

Primary questions	Secondary factors	Tertiary factors
Road conditions OK?	Visibility	Dips in road
		Low car behind hedge
		Reflected sunlight
		Side turnings
	Passing space	Road width
		Road furniture
	Surface grip	Wet leaves
		Damp
		Ice
Can I get past?	Oncoming traffic	Speed assessment
		Distance
	Obstacle car	Speed assessment
		Likely behaviour
	Own car	Gear selected
		Performance ability
Other road users clear?	Traffic behind	Following cars' positioning
		Ability to drop back in
	Obstacles ahead	Pedestrians
		Cyclists
		Side turnings

overtaking. The first column shows the basic questions that have to be answered before committing to overtake. The second column shows the broad considerations behind the basic questions, which break down into specifics in the third column.

You may not agree with the list—in fact it would be very surprising if your own list looked exactly the same—but that only reflects the fact that we all have our own models of experience. You should not fail to be impressed by the fact that the human brain will instantly integrate all these factors and, working from right to left, answer the primary questions. Only if the answers fall within, or reasonably close to, the comfort-zone will the driver go ahead.

Similar models can be constructed for software development projects. See Table 1.2 for an example. Remember that it is only an example, and your own experience may well lead you to add to or subtract from it. Remember also that the human brain will *not* be able to integrate all these factors without a lot of research and analysis. The secondary and tertiary factors are those things that *affect* the primary questions. The primary questions are those significant aspects of the project whereby its success will be measured. For instance, in safety-critical software, 'will reliability objectives be met?' is a primary question, ahead of the much less specific quality question.

This style of table is useful for analysing risk areas, and is used extensively in the rest of the book. Table 1.2 is a very general example only, and is not meant to be representative of all software projects. Another advantage of such a table is that it provides a checklist, and a useful way of integrating all those relatively minor

Risk management for software projects

Table 1.2.   Risk factors in software development

Primary questions	Secondary factors	Tertiary factors
Will the schedule be met?	Estimates	Experience of estimators Methods available
	Code productivity	Skills of people Complexity of code Tools available Aptitude of people
	Dependencies	Use of vendors Internal suppliers
	Test progress	Quality of code Ability of programmers to fix bugs Configuration management
Will quality be acceptable?	Objectives	How well understood? Are they quantified?
	Methods	Defect prevention Defect removal
	Quality management	Independence of assessment Quality records
	Process	Appropriateness Is it enforced?
	Personnel	Quality orientation Training/understanding
Finish within budget?	Overall productivity	Skills Project management
	Resources required	Development machine Staff, materials and overheads
Will function delivered be what is required?	Requirements definition	How up to date? Validated by user?
	User involvement	Project liaison Change management

factors to come up with risk assessments for the primary questions: am I going to finish on time, within budget, and with a product that behaves as the user wants? This table will work for the *software development project*. It will have to be extended to cover business risks.

1.3.2   *Addressing risk*

We have already seen how good we are at managing risk in a complex situation like overtaking. We sum up a lot of factors, and make a judgement about whether to proceed or not; if not, we wait until the circumstances have changed in our favour, helping things along by selecting the right gear, positioning ourselves in the road for maximum visibility, and so on. Only when we feel comfortable about the risk (with respect to the reward) do we make our move. When we go, we watch carefully that the assumptions we started out with are still true: the speed of the oncoming traffic, the road conditions, the absence of pedestrians and cyclists. If anything does go wrong, like the sudden appearance of a car from a side turning that we had not noticed, then we escape from the situation as best we can, and make a note about remembering to scan for inconspicuous side roads in the future. This is a simple set of actions that we perform unconsciously all the time:

- First, we ensure the conditions are as right as we need to feel comfortable with.
- Secondly, we monitor that our judgements were correct as we do what we planned.
- Thirdly, we learn whatever lessons are appropriate.

This is a well-defined, repeatable set of actions that we use all the time, and is called a *process*. A process helps us to deal with difficult situations, because a process represents what we have found to work before. Here, we see a process as a set of unconscious actions. These can be the best processes, when they are so ingrained, but they can also be the worst. Think of them as habits. We all have both good and bad habits. One example of a bad habit is lying-in late on a weekday morning. The reward is immediate; the penalty is having to scramble to get to work on time, with all sorts of attendant risks.

There is an almost exact analogue in software development. It is easy to develop the habit of being lazy early on, of doing an incomplete design, so that coding is started early. The reward is an easy time to start with; the penalty is a scramble to finish on time because the coding is so much harder. The risks are a late finish and poor quality. The good habit to develop is the hard work early on that produces a complete, validated design. The reward is an easy coding phase, with a much better chance of good quality and a finish on time.

Processes are codified good habits. A good software development process is what we see the professionals that we admire doing, and that we all secretly know that *we* should be doing. It means accepting that the rewards will come later, but that they will be all the more worth while for that.

Because most of us know, deep down, that good practice will ensure that work is divided up into trackable units, and each unit is completed before moving on to the next, most people will be familiar with the idea of the cycle being divided up into stages, with activities (or tasks) within stages. Some will also be familiar with the concept of validating each task, and applying entry and exit criteria to it, thus ensuring that at each stage, you are only developing from that which is known to be correct (see Fig. 1.1).

Every developer works to some sort of process. The important question is whether it consists of documented good habits, or undocumented bad habits. It will rarely be the most appropriate process for the job in hand, and (unless it is very well documented, and referenced regularly) it is unlikely that everyone will be working to the same process, even though they may think they are.

As we saw earlier, the reason for a process is that it describes what usually works best, thus saving everyone from having to discover that individually. It represents the encapsulated experience of all who have gone before. There can be no better reason for documenting your process: the amount of wasted effort that it will save

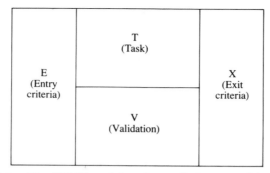

Figure 1.1.   The ETVX model can be applied to an activity, a stage, or a project.

will be orders of magnitude greater than the effort of documenting it properly. Documenting the process has two effects: first, it means that everybody can share your best people's experience and, secondly, it provides a base for moving the process on (improving it). You will need to spend effort in maintaining the process and ensuring that everyone understands and applies it, but still the effort will be less than the wasted effort, and the savings will continue to mount up. *If you have not already done so, document your development process.* Chapter 2 gives more information on how to do this.

When you are planning for risk in software development, you are usually identifying those parts of the process that do not give you sufficient confidence for your particular circumstances. That lack of confidence will be due to a perceived imbalance between risk and reward. What is needed is to:

1   Create the optimum balance between the two,
2   Maintain that balance, and
3   Learn when the balance tips one way or the other.

We call that ideal balance the *optimum risk environment*, the environment in which we feel most comfortable with the perceived risks and rewards. As we said above, any risk reduction activity will cost money, and it is important that the costs and rewards are kept in perspective, so the optimum risk environment is also an *appropriate* risk environment.

It is equally important to remember that everything we do in the project can be regarded as risk management, whether or not we make conscious decisions about them, and as such should be an appropriate response to the circumstances. Thus it may be possible to weaken the process in places, as well as strengthening it in others. For instance, the base process may call for all code to be reviewed or inspected, but for a particularly simple code component, it may be deemed necessary only to inspect the design, and not the code. This decision should be documented, together with the reason: it represents a deviation from the base process, and if the assumptions behind that decision prove to be wrong, we will need to understand why.

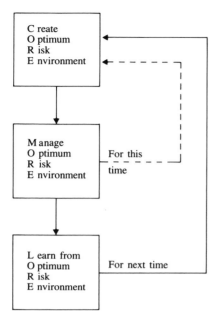

Figure 1.2.   The risk management process loop.

There will be items in the plan other than changes to the process. For example, if there is a risk that the lead technical person may leave during the project, it may be necessary to invest time and training in a replacement, during the early stages of the project.

1.4   Optimum risk management

We saw earlier that *create*, *maintain* and *learn* are the three key elements in the (optimum) risk management process:

1   Create the optimum risk environment (CORE).
2   Manage the optimum risk environment (MORE).
3   Learn from the optimum risk environment (LORE).

The CORE/MORE/LORE process (Fig. 1.2) forms the theme of the rest of this book. In particular, the feedback from the early stages of the project, when managing the early (project definition) stages of the project, will probably lead you to modify your first pass at an optimum risk environment, as you learn more about the real characteristics of the project.

1.4.1   Creating the optimum risk environment — CORE

We saw earlier that the analysis of potential risk areas is an essentially creative activity that will set the tone for the rest of the project. This activity culminates in the production of a risk management plan (RMP) which describes how to bring each risk probability down to (or to stop it developing from) an acceptable level. Developing the RMP is the subject of Chapters 5 and 6.

However, the risks incurred in a project are largely the result of the specific objectives of the product itself. That is why we have included chapters on requirements (from which the objectives are derived) and objectives/specification (Chapters 7 and 8) which determine the targets the product has to meet, and hence the risks.

1.4.2   *Managing the optimum risk environment—MORE*

As with all good processes, the rewards come later. In the case of the risk management process, the MORE stage is where you start to reap the rewards. The CORE stage was the hard work, where the difficult and creative thinking was done, where the negotiations were carried out, and where the RMP was documented. Now is the time that risk-managers should be able to relax a little, and watch their ideas mature into fully grown products. They will know they have been successful if there are no surprises.

In practice, of course, things are never that simple. There will always be things that go wrong that the most meticulous risk managers cannot cater for. However, they can console themselves with the thought that things would have been much worse without the RMP.

Maintaining the ORE is really quite easy. At its simplest it consists of:

1   Tracking that the actions taken to bring the limit-of-performance activities within limits are effective.
2   Tracking that the missing information is being collected, and feeding it back into the RMP.
3   Ensuring that the non-process-related activities are performed.
4   Continually surveying the four primary topics (schedule, cost, quality and function) for evidence of undesirable trends.
5   Managing the odd crisis now and then.

Many readers will recognize this as what most project managers do, but with the emphasis shifted from crisis management to anticipatory management.

The key concept in MORE is tracking and Chapters 9–11 cover tracking within the different stages of a project.

1.4.3   *Learning from the optimum risk environment—LORE*

This is where managers can show what they are made of. Any fool can follow a plan, but it takes a real manager to sit down and analyse what went right, what went wrong, and how it could be prevented from happening again in the future.

It is not a solitary activity, because developing a software product is not a solitary activity. The whole team needs to be involved, because they will all have their own ideas of what was useful and what was not; shortcuts that should have been taken (and were not) or were taken (and should not have been); ideas for preventing problems and ideas for finding problems; and what the manager did wrong (and sometimes even right). All of this information has to be collected, weighed, and sifted.

All who take part will be enriched, the process will be improved, and you will have taken another giant step towards being that elusive creature, the perfect manager. Chapters 12 and 13 tell you how.

1.5   Risk basics summary

In this chapter, we have introduced the concepts of:

- Commitments giving rise to risk
- Processes helping to reduce risk
- Planning to control risk.

To these we must add the concept of measurement, in order to provide a basis for agreement on what has to be achieved, and what has been achieved. In Chapters 2 and 3 we expand these concepts into the development of software.

2
Processes and plans

There is a quotation from Rudyard Kipling that every risk manager should keep permanently displayed. It comes from the story of the Elephant's Child *(Just-So Stories)*, and runs as follows:

> I keep six honest serving-men
>   (They taught me all I knew);
> Their names are What and Why and When
>   And How and Where and Who.

Kipling would have made a great project manager. He has captured the essence of risk management in those four lines. The six questioning words cover all the vital characteristics of the project that the manager has to have under control, and there is even an allusion to the learning from experience that is so important to the building of good mental models.

Processes tend to give you 'What' information, 'When' in the sense of 'in what order', and 'Who' in the sense of 'which function'. The real 'When' (date) and 'Who' information comes in the plan, which allocates real names to the process steps. 'How' is generally described in a detailed procedure. 'Where' does not enter much into software development unless it is intersite or interdepartmental. In a business world, one should add 'How much will it cost?' to this list, to avoid generating the Rolls-Royce of software packages every time.

It is easy to confuse *plans* with other terms that we have already encountered: objective, strategy, process, and procedure. The following list should clarify the differences:

Objective	What you want to achieve.
Strategy	A set of principles, guidelines, and priorities which will lead towards a particular goal, setting up the potential to achieve the goal, but devoid of any concrete activity descriptions.
Process	A high-level definition of the way to achieve a general goal, without attributing personal responsibility for a particular implementation. A series of related activities with inputs and outputs

Procedure

Plan

needed to achieve them. The process is general, and could be followed for any item of the type in question.

A sequential set of instructions for carrying out a task, from a given input point to a desired end point. Details on a particular instance of the procedure are again absent.

A statement of how to proceed in the specific circumstances of the project. A plan is specific about such things as who does what and when, and, by its nature, will have assumptions built into it.

Thus, in risk management terms, a process becomes the best, the most appropriate, approach to achieving an end with minimum risk, while the plan is an implementation of the process, incorporating real-world considerations like productivity rates. Hence the plan is heavily influenced by (and influences) important project characteristics like schedule and cost. Its purpose is to specify the future in more detail, to try and minimize the risk of the unexpected. It is the planner's *model* of what is expected to happen in the future.

The rest of this chapter describes processes and plans in the context of risk management.

2.1   Preparing a process

Good habits do not have a very good press. Good habits are what you learn at your mother's knee; they are perceived as inhibiting and boring, and we are always being told that we should develop more of them. Maybe this is why 'process' (which we characterized in Chapter 1 as 'codified good habits') is often regarded by software developers as something that is there to make life more difficult for them. Say the word 'process', and most people will either yawn or laugh. They will probably think of a large book which sits on a shelf, never changes, and is only brought out to show the auditors, or when someone wants to know what they *have* to do, perhaps to fulfil what they consider to be a totally bureaucratic requirement. Akin, perhaps, to completing a tax return, where there is a set of detailed instructions on paper for working out how much money you are going to lose this year.

But there are other, more friendly, processes in everyday life. Cookery books are one example. First, you decide what kind of meal you want. Then you select the right recipes from the book. You follow the instructions to the letter (processes/procedures), ensuring you have the right ingredients (inputs) and end up with a perfect meal on time (quality deliverable). You rely on the skill of the author of the cookery book, depending only on your own basic cooking techniques.

If you had added ingredients following your own whims and inclinations, the probability is that the meal would have been inedible. *By following the process, the risk is reduced* to the point that it is likely that the meal will be enjoyable. Later on, when you are more experienced, you *can* experiment, you may even write notes on the recipe of what you did differently to make it taste even better, so you can reuse the idea again another time (this is process improvement, to which we will return later), and eventually make up your own recipes.

This chapter is all about the role of process in risk management. We saw in the first chapter that the basic strategies for risk control are:

- Provide support (where you are at the limits of performance)
- Collect information (where you have to cope with unknowns)

A process usually needs to be tailored to cope with specific project risks. It is rare that a base development process remains unaltered for a software project. Perhaps this is a follow-on release, so you do not need to do the system design the second time around. Perhaps the project is short, cheap, and low risk, so you do not need all the checkpoints. Perhaps it is PC rather than mainframe, and the distribution mechanism is different. This does not make the process any less valuable. You take a set of intelligent decisions based on your particular product circumstances, and tailor the process to suit your project. As you do, you can start on the project management task of deciding who will execute each process step, and when.

Some may object that a development process should be sacrosanct, as in the case of safety-critical systems, for instance. Once you have established the appropriate process, then of course it should be sacrosanct—but it is unlikely that every one of your safety-critical systems needs exactly the same process. Tailoring ensures that the appropriate process is used for every project.

2.1.1 *Characterizing process*

Our description of process as a set of codified good habits needs some expansion: 'codified' means 'communicable in a rigorous self-consistent way'; 'good habits' implies that we want something done that way always. So a more complete definition of process is 'a definable, repeatable, measurable sequence of tasks which produce a quality product for the customer'. Definable, in that you could explain it to someone else; repeatable and predictable, in that you can run it a second time and achieve the same result; and measurable, in that you can measure what it has achieved, and what it took to achieve it (this is essential for process improvement).

A process describes 'what' and 'in what order', and possibly 'with what sort of people and tools'. At a lower level comes the procedure, which tells you 'how'. Note that the procedure should be capable of being followed by a newcomer who has the basic skills. Importantly, the state you are trying to reach with the process should fulfil one of your job objectives.

A process is a well-run workshop floor, where apprentices can produce results comparable to that of the master craftsperson. They may do it slower and they may need help with the more difficult pieces, but with the basic skills in place, they can follow the good habits developed over the years by their mentors, and all of their predecessors, to produce good, repeatable results. 'Basic skills', for a software developer, are the intellectual equivalent of the muscle-memory that a craftsperson develops working with tools.

Note that nothing has been said about paper being the essential way of delivering the process to its customers. 'Consult your local guru' can be a valid piece of process, as long as you have defined the guru's skill level and given the guru job objectives to be one. Probably the most effective process is the one where the work is done within a machine environment which embodies the process, that is, you can only complete the work by following the process.

In summary, a process:

- Tells you (at least) what to do, in what order
- Is well-defined, repeatable, predictable, and measurable
- Will consist of different related activities
- Will help you meet your job objectives

whereas a procedure:

- Tells you how to do part of the process
- Can be repeated by anyone with the basic skills

All of the foregoing has a number of implications for process:

- It must be fit-for-purpose.
- It should consist of simple interrelated steps.
- It must be capable of improvement, to keep it up-to-date.
- It should be supported by tools.

Each of these four points is now discussed in more detail.

Fit-for-purpose

An acceptable process should have a number of key attributes:

1 It should have an objective, stated up front: 'This process will help you to . . .'. This objective should clearly relate to your business objective, to the job objectives you give your project team, and to the project objectives. In that way, the team will see that the process will help them do what you pay them for, and that should encourage them to use it.
2 It should delight its customers—the people who will use it. It should tell them what they need to know to do their job, and require a minimum of extra effort from them to fulfil other team needs—the provision of management control information, and so on. Process is ideal for documenting and even automating

the mundane trivia and releasing your project team to focus on those risk areas which really need their skills.

3 It should be delivered in the form which the users will find most helpful: for instance, it could be online, on paper, a resident expert or (ideally) delivered as an environment in which the process users (the software developers) will be presented with appropriate work alternatives as they proceed. Data or measures needed for control should be gathered by the system monitoring what the developers do. A stepping-stone on the way to this ideal, which we have found works well, is an online process held as a large network of small files linked together in hypertext fashion. Readers can access information in development sequence, by activity type, or by alphabetic reference.

4 Ideally, it should be based on experience, not necessarily yours. If you have no access to experience, as a last resort you can use your common sense and imagination to invent and document your own. This will certainly be better than nothing at all, and you will have a chance to measure and improve for next time, denied you if you just work from your head.

Inter-related steps

It is not so much a risk as a racing certainty that unless you break your perception of the project down into small areas, each of which you can grasp and understand, you will not be able to control the costs, the delivery time, or even the function delivered. This is just as true of the small project of a few person-years as it is of the 200-person project that takes two or more years.

This section tells you some ways you might divide your project so that you can understand and control it, and thus reduce the risk.

Checkpoints

Checkpoints can be a useful way to break the project lengthwise, typically into three stages, each ended by a checkpoint meeting. Checkpoints impose financial constraints and commit only small amounts of funding in the early stages, while more is learned about the requirements and technical feasibility of the product—and hence the costs. This reduces the risk of pouring good money after bad. Only if the product is still an attractive proposition in light of the increased knowledge is the go-ahead given to proceed to the next stage. The checkpoint meeting has a higher level of management involvement than other project meetings, including financial people who can pull the financial plug if they are not happy.

The three stages might be called:

- Initial proposal
- Planning and commitment
- Development

These are what we use in our own environment, and have worked for us. They will not necessarily be right for you. We are using these (and later examples) for illustrative purposes, to show the important principles.

During the first stage, an amount of money is allocated to draw up a business proposal for the system. The team would be asked to go away, spend no more than a certain amount (about 10 per cent of the expected total project cost) and come back with a proposal, including:

- Summary of requirements
- Quantified product objectives
- Assessment of competition
- Dependencies (outside project span of control)
- Tentative schedule
- Costs, expected sales, and revenues
- Detailed plan to reach next checkpoint

This would be presented to senior management who would then give the go-ahead to proceed to the next checkpoint, or not, as the case may be.

The team would be instructed to spend up to another 20 per cent of the project cost and come back with an agreed detailed specification, plans from the entire team showing how they planned to develop and test the product, and a commitment to deliver it by the required end date. During this stage, prototyping and design would occur, and all participants would need to get together to agree a coherent set of plans, to be staffed with real people. There then would follow the second checkpoint at which management agreed or not to hand over the final 70 per cent of the money to deliver the product.

The final checkpoint would ensure that the product had been developed as planned and was available on time.

There is obviously scope to hold other checkpoints during the final phase, but if you do, be sure that you know what it is you expect to see. Meetings where the team roll up and just tell you where they are can be confusing and unproductive.

Stages

These are effectively lengthwise breakdowns of the project at the next level down, for the benefit of the product manager. Each of these stages delivers a well-defined work product. This enables the risk manager to determine whether the risks are materializing of function, quality, schedule, and cost objectives not being met.

The business proposal phase can usefully divide into two stages:

- Requirements definition
- Solution (objectives) definition

running sequentially.

The planning and commitment phase (in a conventional development) would be divided into three stages:

- High-level design
- Low-level design
- Component-level design

The development phase would include:

- Code
- Unit test
- Function verification
- Product verification
- System verification
- Packaging
- Customer field test

These are components, or stages, of a process that we have identified as a starting point. Most significant projects require these stages, but they have to be tailored into the right sort of process for the project. This tailoring has to take into account the people involved, the tools available, and (most of all) the risks to be managed.

Activities, tasks, and completion

Stages are far too coarse a division of a project for adequate control. Further subdividing will lead to activities and tasks, against which you can confidently measure progress. One word of warning about a traditional software risk, the '90 per cent complete' syndrome. Ask programmers how they are getting on, and popular wisdom has it that you will be told that the program is 90 per cent complete, and will be finished next week. When you ask again next week, you will be told the same. The way round this is never to ask how finished anything is. Divide things up into a number of smaller items so that they clearly are finished, or not. Programs, for example come in the sequence:

- Coded
- Inspection called
- Inspection held
- Defects fixed
- Ready for unit test

Each one of these is binary. Dividing the project small enough allows you never to have to ask how finished something is. By the usual rule of thumb, 'small enough' means about one person-week's effort.

Process improvement

As we said earlier, if processes are left to stagnate, they become increasingly irrelevant, and people stop using them. You can reduce this risk by holding review meetings at the end of the project, as described in a later chapter. Findings from the review are fed back into the process to improve it for next time. But at the lower level, you can get your process improvements to the process customers even faster using causal analysis techniques. You can put as much or as little effort into this as you like, but as with all things, it is as well to measure the cost and the benefit as you go along, so that you know when you are not being effective.

Without going into the full details of the technique here, the idea is to take a regular look at problems which the developers introduce (code errors, design errors, or whatever), and pick out the most common or the most costly problems since you last met. These then become the subject of a causal analysis meeting, at which the reasons for perpetrating the errors are explored by a team which includes the perpetrators. These are egoless meetings, at which there is no punishment for admitting errors. After all, the errors came from using a process, so you can blame the process owner, who will have broader shoulders than anyone else. Action team meetings then determine what action is required and make it happen. Often this will be to make improvements to the process. The cycle time on this complete activity is only a few weeks, so experience can be quickly fed back into the system for the benefit of others.

If this all sounds rather costly, it is worth remembering that the cost of fixing a defect is incurred for *every* defect. The cost of defect prevention activity occurs only once for each *class* of defect. Once the process or procedures are updated, you should never incur the cost of fixing that kind of defect again. So although apparently costly, defect prevention is clearly an investment activity which shows high returns during the life of the current project development. See Humphrey (1989) for more details.

Causal analysis supplements, but does not replace, the standard process improvement cycle (see Fig. 1.2). The process has objectives, measures, and metrics, and by comparing actuals with plan when you use the process, you can feed back information to secure process improvement.

It is worth saying here that the process owner is the person responsible for ensuring that the process truly meets the needs of its users. In practice, this means keeping it up to date through the medium of experience-gathering meetings, such as those just referred to.

Tools and techniques

Doing anything for the first time without assistance is more risky than doing it the second or third time. Performing mundane tasks is boring, concentration can be lost and mistakes made. Tools, which save you from boring jobs and help you do things right, can therefore be thought of as risk-reduction mechanisms. Techniques for developing good quality software can also help. Examples include:

- Library systems
- Project control systems
- Formal design languages
- Cleanroom (see Green *et al.*, 1990)
- Prototyping
- Checklists
- Small teams
- Small programs
- Configuration management
- Reuse of design and code which has been proven

This is not the place to describe the relative merits of different tools and techniques. It is for you to decide which best meet your needs, and to build them into your procedures. There is, of course, a learning curve associated with all new tools or methods, so ensure that any tools you use are really relevant to your objectives. You would not use a chisel to drive a screw. Do not use tools for their own sake—make sure they are tools which will help. You do not use a word processor to leave a note for the milkman.

Remember that the reuse technique can be applied to other things as well as design/code. The reuse concept must be extended to include experience. Every tool, method, and technique should have an owner who should collect all experience resulting from the use of them. The pooled experience should be made available to all, and used to plan improvements to the organization's toolkit.

2.2 Preparing and using a plan

In this section, we present some guidance on plan content and using the plan to minimize risk.

2.2.1 Plan content

Although plans are all very different, it is possible to give some general guidance as to what you should look for when writing a plan, of any kind. (Similar guidance can be followed if you ever have to review someone else's plan.)

In general, of course, a plan describes how the work is to be done that accomplishes the project's objectives. It must also include activities that implement the risk management strategies of providing support and/or collecting information. A list of all the important plan elements and requirements is given in Appendix 4.

In our experience, most plans are more akin to strategies, and all manner of plausible reasons are advanced to defend them. If you see a plan like that too, that is a *risk*, because the project has not been thought through properly. The theme running through this book is that real thinking is necessary to control risk; where lack of thinking is self-evident, warning lights should start flashing.

2.2.2   *Deliverables outside your span of control*

As we said earlier, when you construct a plan, you are putting your expectations into more concrete form: the plans express what you expect to happen under your control. There will often be circumstances when you have a dependency on others over whom you have no direct control. This dependency will be a deliverable of some kind, whether of a product delivered under agreed circumstances, or of a service that has to meet agreed criteria. You cannot prepare plans for the other party, but you can make sure that there is no possible scope for misinterpretation between you. The terms that we use are:

- Document of understanding (DOU) for a product deliverable, and
- Service-level agreement (SLA) for the provision of some sort of service

By making the exact terms of the agreement clear and explicit, you minimize the risk of your expectations not being met. You can also specify any information that you need from the other party so that you can monitor that your expectations are still likely to be met. See Appendices 6 and 7 for a list of the items for consideration for inclusion in the documents.

As with all plans, the norm should be that the reality is according to plan. The emphasis with all status reporting must be that deviations from the plan are unacceptable; the response from the owner of the deviating item should be to report the deviation, and the steps being taken to get back on target. Deviations from plans must be honestly reported, status reporting must occur at regular intervals, and any change to the plan must be tightly controlled.

Tracking a DOU is harder than tracking a project. By definition, you are not in control, and are probably remote from where the work is actually being done. The three main failings of DOUs that we have been involved with have been:

- Failure to get them off the ground properly, to liaise with the right people, to get proper management agreement that there should be a DOU at all, or to get it signed off in time to be of practical use

This should be tackled at the risk planning stage (see later) when the dependency on another party for a deliverable will almost certainly be identified as a risk.

Putting a DOU in place will be an early action identified in your risk management plan.

- Failure to agree and enforce function and quality standards for deliverables

It is up to you to decide what the quality requirements are for the piece of work you have contracted out, in exactly the same way as for any other deliverable. They should be specified clearly in the agreement, with targets, how they are to be measured, and the data that should be provided. There is more information on this in Chapter 3.

- Failure to get honest tracking information from the other party

Be business-like. Make visits to understand the process used, hold regular reviews where appropriate, check random samples to ensure that the data you are given is truly representative, and make payments based on staged deliverables meeting quality criteria.

A SLA covers more mundane concerns that nevertheless affect your chances of success. First, who are your suppliers? Who delivers things to you? (Simple things like furniture, computer equipment, etc.) Secondly, there is another bunch of more nebulous items that you tend to take for granted, but you actually depend on to do your job. If they were ever taken away, your project would sink. An example of this is your mainframe computer service, run by another department, outside your span of control. Depending on your assessment of the risk in the service provided, you could undertake a 'service-level agreement' so that you are clear from the start what will be provided for you during development, how you will measure it, and what you will do if fails to meet expectations.

2.3   Using the plan

In an ideal situation, all the activities will take place by the dates agreed. The better your mental models when preparing the plans, the more likely they are to happen. Actual progress can be checked at a regular tracking meeting, say once a fortnight. All that need be reported are deviations from the plan and how the perpetrator of the deviation plans to get back on course. This includes your own risk management work!

It is worth highlighting here the difference between progress meetings, status meetings, and tracking meetings. At a *progress* meeting, developers stand up and tell you what they want to tell you—all sorts of sob stories about the problems they have had with a particular item, why they have not been able to finish it in spite of working till midnight every night, and so on. At a *status* meeting, they stand up and tell you where they are and what items they completed last week, but not how this relates to the plan of what they were supposed to be doing. At a *tracking* meeting, every activity is compared with the plan, and only deviations are presented.

Too often, tracking appears to be used in the scouting sense—picking up trails and following the project wherever it goes and finally arriving at the destination hours after the project did. A railway analogy is better: you expect the train to run on certain tracks, if it does not, there needs to be the fullest possible investigation!

2.3.1 Tracking risks

There are two risks involved in tracking which can be totally eliminated if you think about them beforehand. The first one is that you do not get real information from the data presented. 'The number of defects found is 573' is a piece of data. Information, on the other hand, is data which has been selected, processed, and presented in such a way that you are able to take an immediate decision on it related to your business goals.

At a tracking meeting, would you rather be told:

- We have found 273 defects.
- Seventeen of them were show-stoppers.
- We are raising defects at the rate of 17 per day.
- The test team have put in 20 hours overtime each in the last week.
- Of the 809 test cases run, 182 have found errors.
- Of the defects found, 27 per cent have been closed, 38 per cent are in fix status, and the rest are open.

Or would you rather be told how many weeks before the test is complete? Almost certainly the latter, and that is the way we are in real life. But in the workplace we become fascinated by pretty charts and the masses of complicated data we have gathered, and our minds stray from the real reason for doing the tracking and presenting the chart.

The *thinking* should go in the following sequence:

1 What am I trying to achieve? (objectives)
2 What is my expectation along the way? (plans, models)
3 How might reality differ from this expectation? (risk analysis)
4 What corrective action might I want to take? (risk planning)
5 Therefore, what specific information do I need to be able to take the decision? (risk management)

Ensure that your tracking charts give you that information, as you want it, with no further interpretation needed.

The second risk is that you may end up seeing data (and information derived from it) which is not what you think it is. This could be deliberate—the team could be trying to hide something from you—or it could be accidental. Either way, the more automation there can be in data collection, the better. For example, if you have a library system to which programs are sent when complete, let it record when the programs come in, and the subsequent change activity. Do not ask the developers for such data separately: it is irritating to be asked for something which could be quite easily discovered, and the developers may be tempted to stretch the truth if things are going badly (remember the 90 per cent complete syndrome).

2.3.2   *Changing a plan*

There will inevitably be times when the actuals are so far away from the plan that it needs to be changed. This does not mean that the plan was a failure. What it tells you is that the assumptions that you made when you built the plan are no longer valid. This is a perfectly normal situation, and reflects a fact of life in the real world: things change. Do not feel bad about having to change the plan: rather, feel proud that your plan is a working document that describes the way things are. This does not mean that you have *carte blanche* to change the end date at the first hint of a slip in the schedule. What it does mean is that the managerial skills that you bring to the problem should be expressed and communicated through an updated plan.

A few considerations:

1   All changes *must* be done with the knowledge and involvement of the whole team—it is they who have to carry it out.
2   Resist changing the plan at every meeting—if the plan is totally fluid, it will soon lapse into disrepute.
3   Keep all previous instances of the plan—it is very instructive to track the plan changes over time, and this can only be done when plan versions are kept as historical records.

3
Numbers

3.1 In measured terms

Lord Kelvin said: 'You can't know what you can't measure'. Today, this has become a rather hackneyed phrase, though for the best possible reason: it has some enduring truth in it. Lord Kelvin's dictum is particularly true of elusive concepts like *quality*. Quality, for developers, is doomed to remain an unattainable will-o'-the-wisp unless it is quantified. The customers, of course, will form their own opinions in the end, which will be expressed in the form of a binary 'buy/do not buy' decision, because quality is usually more easily recognized by its absence than its presence.

The idea of quality in software is obviously important. People will discuss it at length, but rarely to any advantage, because they do not have any common ground for comparison of 'good', 'bad', 'better', and 'worse'. A metric provides that common ground: it is the quantification of a *useful* idea or concept. We stress the 'useful', because a metric is of no use unless it supports the achievement of some important characteristic of the project. Unfortunately, the usefulness of a metric is often subjugated to the ease of measurement: a metric is put in place simply because something is easily measured. Using metrics just for the sake of some numbers lays you open to the charge of bean-counting and the derision of those doing useful work.

A typical example of an easily measured metric is lines of code (LOC). This is often used as a measure of size of the problem: first as an estimate, and finally as a measure of the work done. The difficulty is that LOC is a better measure of the solution than the problem, and even as a measure of the solution, it has considerable weaknesses. That is not to say that the LOC metric should be avoided entirely: it has its uses, and one of them is illustrated later in this chapter. LOC is not, however, a good measure of the amount of problem to be solved. Here, a useful concept is that of *function*, or *capability*. The user gets delivery of some capability that removes the problem—the technical means of the solution (100 LOC of APL, 1000 LOC of COBOL, or 50 LOC of 4GL) are irrelevant and meaningless if they all solve the same problem.

The useful concept of function can be quantified by the use of some technique such as *function points*, first developed by Al Albrecht of IBM. Function points attempt to measure the size of the user's problem, and provide a rather more technology-independent way of estimating and comparing productivities than LOC.

The LOC is an example of a metric that is a *measure*, that is, it can be applied directly to the idea that you are interested in, in the same way that a ruler is held against a line to measure its length. There is, though, another kind of metric: the *indicator*. An indicator is not directly attributable to the interesting idea: you can only infer the information that you want. Function points are an indicator: a composite number derived from a number of different factors which indirectly measure function.

Another example of the difference between a measure and an indicator is in measuring the reliability of a product on customers' premises. It is extremely expensive to do multiple reliability measurements to find out if the product is meeting its design targets in the field, but much cheaper and easier to collect customer satisfaction survey data on reliability. The customer satisfaction index is an indicator, whereas mean time to failure (MTTF) is a measure.

There are two other important characteristics of a metric. First, it should actually be measurable. A risk manager might find it useful to know the experience of programmers. (It might for instance be useful to try to correlate productivity or defects-committed with a programmer's experience.) But experience relates to what one has learnt from what one has actually achieved, which makes measuring program function look like child's play. Experience is such a vague concept that it is fundamentally unquantifiable. Far better to lower one's sights, and pick some characteristic that can be quantified, such as weeks of technical IT education. Though not a measure of experience, it is an indicator, and can be accurately quantified.

The second characteristic is that the metric should be defensible. If a metric is truly useful (that is, it puts you in control and lowers the risk of something), the numbers will inevitably be challenged by those affected by the control. This means that the numbers have to be defended, and hence must be credible: they must be as precise and as reliable as the collection system allows. Make sure that the data collection system works, and works *all* the time.

In the rest of this chapter, we look at how metrics can be used in the setting, tracking, and achievement of project objectives. At the end of the chapter, there is an outline for a quality plan that shows how to document quality targets and the steps that will be taken to achieve them.

3.2   Commitments and quality

We saw in Chapter 1 that it is at the making of a commitment that risks are established. It is only when the software project manager promises to deliver something that the attendant risks begin to mean anything. The important word here is 'something'. It is tempting to believe that if one is not too specific about what is being delivered, the risk is correspondingly less. Nothing could be further from the truth. The customers have their own expectations of what is to be delivered to them, and the less specific one is, the more likely that their expectations will not be met.

The answer is, of course (how easy it is to say it!), to find out what the customers' real requirements are, to involve them in deciding what can and cannot be delivered (including when, and at what cost) and to set targets for what is to be delivered. (We shall call them objectives from now on.) The risks then are specific ones relating to the objectives, rather than one huge risk of a totally dissatisfied set of customers. It is much easier to manage a set of many smaller individual known risks than the unspecified big one of the customer perceiving a poor quality product. This raises two important questions: who is 'the customer', and what do we mean by 'quality'?

It is usual to think of 'the customer' as the person who hands over the cash, but it may also be the person who actually has to sit down and use what has been delivered. In a domestic situation they are often the same person. For software, it is much more complicated. Usually, the person who pays for it is different from the person who has to install it, who is different from the person who actually has to use it, who is different from the person who fixes the defects found in it.

Each of these customer-types will have their own specific needs, and provided those needs are met, they will perceive the product as being 'of good quality'. So quality is 'whatever property satisfies the real needs of the customers'. That is not an original quote, but its attribution is lost in the mists of antiquity (in computing terms). There are some implications in this simple statement: that we have established what the customers *really* want and have *verified* it with them, and that we know the full extent of our customer set.

Too often, software quality is taken to mean simply a 'low level of defects' (where 'defect' means 'bug' or 'a way in which the deliverable failed to match its specification'), but that is closer to the definition of reliability. Quality is a much broader term. If, however, you ask people what is really important to them about the way the product behaves then you will start to collect some more specific answers. These tend to coalesce into categories which are more easily defined, and can be given some objective measures. The set of categories offered here is called the 'abilities', for obvious reasons.

Capability	The functions that the product offers.
Usability	How easy it is to exploit the capability.
Performance	The speed at which the capability is delivered, including factors like response time, execution speed and use of resources, as perceived by customers in their environment.
Installability	How easily the product can be up and running, including

	factors like the effort it takes, and the level of skill needed to achieve this.
Reliability	How often it fails to deliver the capability you want, and the way it fails—gracefully, or incomprehensibly?
Maintainability	How easily a failure can be sorted out, including factors like how long it takes, and how much it costs.
Learnability	How long it takes users to become confident with your new product. Consider existing users and new users separately.
Migratability	How long/how much effort it takes you to migrate from your existing way of working to working with the new product. Will there be a massive data conversion job?
Compatibility	The degree of compatibility between your product and others.
Extendability	How easy it will be to extend the system later.
Environments	Where it will work.
Cost	How much it will cost the customer.
Profitability	Self-explanatory.
Marketability	The attractiveness to the customer of the product in the marketplace.

Note that some of these, such as usability, usually require further subdivision before they can be specified and measured unambiguously.

IBM uses a set known by the acronym CUPRIMD, which stands for capability, usability, performance, reliability, installability, maintainability, and documentation. This list may not work for everyone (for instance, documentation is perhaps not a quality but a solution) but it is a good representative set of the software characteristics in which customers are interested. Many people will want to adapt the list to their own circumstances. If your system is so good that you can find all you need to know about it without documentation, that is fine, and there is no good reason to measure documentation especially. Learnability and referability may be better alternatives.

Having arrived at your own version of this set, it can be used as a checklist when looking at many stages of the project development.

3.3   Quality metrics

In the previous section, we discussed the different attributes that make up the concept of quality. Each of these attributes can be quantified, some in many different ways, and the usefulness of the metric will vary according to who uses it. See Table 3.1 for some examples. The table contains measurement areas, rather than specific measures (deliberately, as we shall see), and introduces the idea of different audiences for the measure through a *beneficiary* of the information conveyed by the metric.

In Table 3.1, no corresponding metrics have been suggested. This is deliberate—it is not that we have none to offer, but the metrics should reflect what

Table 3.1. Measurement areas for quality attributes

Attribute	Metric areas	Beneficiary
Capability	Functionality delivered versus requirements	User
	Volume of function to deliver	Development
Usability	Ease of learning important tasks	User
	Ease of completing a task	User
	Intuitiveness	User
Performance	Transaction throughput	User
	Response time to an enquiry	User
	Size of machine needed to run the product	User
Reliability	Mean time between failures	User
	Number of defects	Development
	Severity of defects	User
	Severity/impact of failures	User
Installability	Ease of making product available to use	User/system programmer
	Time to complete installation	User/system programmer
	Skill level needed by installer	User/system programmer
Maintainability	Ease of problem diagnosis	Development
	Ease of fixing problem correctly	Development
Documentation	Ease of understanding	User
	Ease of finding relevant information	User
	Completeness of information	User

is important in your particular circumstances. For instance, under 'documentation', we have a metric of 'ease of understanding'. Depending on the circumstances, the appropriate metric could be:

- The coverage of different national languages supported among the user population
- The maximum reading age of the text (measured by a text analyser)
- The proportion of graphics to text, in terms of page space

All of these are indicators of ease of understanding; they are all eminently measurable (with the right tools), and provide useful information in the appropriate circumstances.

In general, quality (indeed, all software) metrics tend to be of the following types:

- *Time*   The time taken to achieve something, (often used in usability metrics), or between events, as in mean time between failures.
- *Probability*   The likelihood of an event in a defined environment. A very useful type of metric, as just about every useful characteristic can be expressed as a probability, but the effort of collecting statistically significant data can be prohibitive.
- *Proportion*   A catch-all: the ratio of two simple counts, such as defects per thousand lines of source code. (Defects as a quality metric is discussed in more detail below.) A ratio is useful because it gives a reflection of quality as a whole, or normalizes to some standard size.

Often, the basic types will be combined, as in a metric for maintainability: 'the probability that reported problems will be diagnosed, fixed, and tested in less than five working hours by junior programmers and above, who are unfamiliar with the relevant code'.

3.3.1   Defects as a quality metric

The one piece of data that seems to be common to most development organiz- ations is a count of bugs, errors, defects—call them what you will. *Webster's 9th New Collegiate Dictionary* defines a defect as 'an imperfection that impairs worth' and 'a lack of something necessary for completeness, adequacy or perfection'. A defect, then, is rather more than a simple program bug. Poor performance, lack of usability, unmaintainable code, etc. all may be classed as defects, contributing to a defective product. A prerequisite to measuring defects is being able to identify them. How do we do this in an objective manner?

The same dictionary also defines defective as 'falling below the norm in structure'. This gives the answer. A software defect is an undesirable variance from the 'norm', that is, the planned structure for that software. A defective specification is one that 'lacks something necessary for completeness, adequacy or perfection' when related to the norm defined for it by the program objectives. A defective piece of code is one that 'lacks something necessary for completeness, adequacy or perfection' when related to the norm defined for it by the design for that piece of code. In this instance, 'the defect' is 'that which is lacking'.

This means in practice that any metrics programme based on measuring and analysing defects is doomed to failure unless norms—plans, designs, specifications—have been established in the first place, for it is only by comparing actuals against plans that a defect can be identified as such. (It is important not to be deflected by considerations of software development ideologies here. Planning is as relevant to rapid prototyping as it is to the waterfall process model. If you do not know where you are going, how do you know when you have got there? See Chapter 5 for more on managing risk by planning.)

This explains why formal inspection techniques (Fagan, 1986) are so successful. They methodically compare 'successor' documents with their progenitors. For example:

Progenitor	*Successor*
Specification	Design
Design	Code
Requirements definition	System test plan
Specification	Functional test plan
Design	Unit test plan

Any inconsistency between the two is pursued as a potential defect.

3.4   Tracking achievement of objectives

The previous section was about attaching metrics to important qualities, or attributes, of your product. The corollary is that, with a metric, you can define a target figure for that metric. Thus, for the maintainability metric example in the previous section, it might be reasonable to set a target of 90 per cent of problems fixed under the stated conditions. The risk manager now has a commitment which cannot be verified as met until the product is in the field. How can the risk manager be assured that the risk is under control during the earlier stages? The *thinking* should follow this sequence:

1   What are the reasonable expectations along the way? (plans, models)
2   How might reality differ from expectations? (risk analysis)
3   What information is needed to make decisions?

In the maintainability example, the following plans might be put in place (as a simple example only) with the reasonable expectation that, together, they will achieve the target:

- Use a design methodology that delivers code modules of less than 50 LOC.
- Each module is to have a comprehensive prologue box, and the code is to be heavily commented.
- During testing, a sample of problems will be fixed by programmers other than the code owner, under the target conditions.

During the development stages, the risk manager needs to know if these plans are being realized. The following metrics and targets might be defined by the risk managers as a means of tracking that reality matches expectations:

- The design stage is to have 100 per cent review coverage of design units, with the review leader to sign-off that units meet the criteria
- The code stage is to employ a code analysis tool that will check that 100 per cent of code units have the standard prologue box, and there is a minimum of 1 comment line to each 5 LOC.
- The test manager is to allocate a representative sample of 10 per cent of bugs found during testing to other than the unit's owner; 90 per cent of those bugs should be fixed in less than 5 hours of working time.

The risk manager now has a handle on the risk, and has three separate chances to correct any out-of-line situation during development, before the problem is found in the field.

A more quantitative example is given in the case study at the end of this chapter.

3.5   Quality plans

The formal mechanism for defining quality objectives is the quality plan. It may come as some surprise when we suggest that this should also be the formal medium through which progress against those objectives is tracked. The reasoning is as follows. Quality objectives have to be set, then documented for all to see. What then? All too often, quality tracking begins—if it begins at all—without much further reference to the original plan. Only at the end of development, or at least an embarrassingly long way into it, do we discover that we are some way from meeting the targets that were set.

This means that a quality plan has to become a 'living' document; a document that is not simply prepared once and forgotten about, but a document that is updated frequently. This has implications for the style of quality plan that we are talking about. It is far removed from the quality plan which is not so much a plan as a collection of pious hopes and good intentions, committed to paper for the sole purpose of satisfying some bureaucratic requirement, the good sense of which has long since been forgotten. A quality plan has to be centred on the proposed metrics programme. It must define :

- The various quality targets, in quantified terms, for the product
- The quality development techniques that will be followed in order to meet those targets
- The quality measurements that will be made so that progress towards the quality targets can be assessed

Let us examine each of these in a little more detail.

3.5.1   Quality targets

Our concern is to set quantifiable targets for each aspect of our product's quality. We may be using the CUPRIMD set mentioned earlier in this chapter, or we may be using another set, more suitable to our need. What is important is that each has an appropriate target set for it in the quality plan.

What is appropriate? That will depend on who the beneficiary of the quality objective is—user, developer, tester, etc. It means that three types of target need to be considered.

1   Customer view targets

What quality targets need to be set to satisfy the customers for our product? Some will inevitably be more important than others. We need to know what they are, and this should (but often does not) form a key element of the activity of requirements' gathering.

Some techniques, such as the quality function deployment technique in Chapter 8, lend themselves readily to the identification of such customer view targets.

2   Postprocess targets

What do we, as software developers, need to aim for in terms of quality? The set will not be the same as that for the customer view. To take a simple example, where the customer may be most concerned with MTTF, the developer is likely to be more concerned with the number of latent defects in the product, for it is these that will most affect the level of postship support that has to be provided.

Postprocess targets, then, are primarily concerned with the developer's intentions for the finished software. Is there going to be a follow-on release? If so, quality criteria such as maintainability (code complexity, internal documentation, etc.) will need to have targets set which are very different to those for the customer.

3 Inprocess targets

Both customer view and postprocess targets are 'after the event' targets—they relate to the finished product. Our concern, naturally enough, is that those targets are met. The risk we run is that they will not be. The function of inprocess targets is to minimize that risk.

An in-process target is an intermediate target. It can relate directly to either a customer view or postprocess metric, or it can be different but supportive of the premise that we are on track to meet those targets—it can be an indicator, in other words. Thus, code growth against plan of less than 5 per cent might be an inprocess target. While not a target that either a customer or a future developer would be interested in knowing about, its achievement during code development would be a good indicator that, for instance, the postprocess and customer view targets for code complexity and maintainability were likely to be met at the end of the day. See Sec. 3.6 for an example of inprocess targets.

3.5.2 Quality development techniques

A quality technique is an indicator. If followed, it indicates that quality in one or more of our attributable areas should be positively affected. Conversely, if not followed, it indicates, not that quality will be bad, but that there are no sound reasons for expecting it to be good either!

A simple way of focusing the mind on good practices is to list them in the quality plan and require reasons for their not being used. This provides the necessary check on the development process without removing the freedom for the project manager to tailor that process as necessary.

The following technique outline is all that is needed. A (series of) checkboxes list those techniques currently recognized as being consistent with good software quality. In the quality plan, the project manager indicates the extent to which each practice is going to be employed on a scale of 1 to 5, thus:

1 Not being used at all
2 Ad hoc use
3 Used in selected areas

4   Considerable use
5   Fundamental to development process

A representative (but not exhaustive) list of candidate techniques might be as shown in Fig. 3.1.

Finally, and as a helpful way of recording new quality initiatives, a table should be included to provide the opportunity for the project manager to indicate new or original quality techniques that are being followed for this particular project (see 'quality initiatives' table in Fig. 3.1).

A useful additional section to have here is that of 'deviations from quality techniques'. Although smacking a little of 'big brother', if adherence to the stated quality techniques is company policy then some statement as to why any particular technique has been flagged as a 1 (not used at all) is worth recording. If the deviation proves to have been a mistake, then that is a lesson learned for next time (assuming there is a next time, that is—it depends on the extent of the nosedive taken by quality as a result of the deviation). If, on the other hand, the deviation proves to have been a valid action to take then that, too, is a lesson for the future—are we requiring all of our product developments to do work which results in little or no improvement to quality?

3.5.3   *Quality measures*

In this section the quality plan details the type of measurements that will be taken in support of each of its targets. It also provides templates for up-to-date figures to be inserted so that, at any time, the plan is an accurate reflection of current progress towards those targets.

Warning: this section can become extensive, if done properly. For instance, if following the CUPRIMD model for quality attributes we would, in this section, effectively be completing a quality measurement 3×7 matrix (Table 3.2) in which every cell references that part of the quality plan which describes:

- Nature of the measurement
- Justification
- How the data is to be collected
- How it is to be presented

As an abbreviated example, the following might be part of this section for the quality attribute of reliability.

Example—customer view reliability measures

Reliability for product X will be assessed in terms of field defects, user problems reported per user month, and MTTF. The targets for reliability are to achieve an

THE SOFTWARE QUALITY BASICS

Techniques	1	2	3	4	5
Development process defined, documented, inspectable					
Verification: design through simulation, analysis, and early prototypes, product validation throughout the cycle					
Inprocess measurements and ratings: track/predict quality and cycle times, demonstrates ever-improving goals					
Defect causal analysis and prevention					
Robust change control/problem management					
Reuse: of code/design and knowledge/experience					

GOOD PROGRAMMING PRACTICES

Techniques	1	2	3	4	5
Use of historical data					
Early customer involvement					
Quality management process					
Single development team throughout the development cycle					
Customer user-error causal analysis					
Software reuse					
Customer view of quality					
Prototypes to customers					

SOFTWARE DEVELOPMENT TECHNIQUES

Techniques	1	2	3	4	5
'Cleanroom' software development					
Formal design languages					

REQUIREMENTS, SPECIFICATION AND DESIGN AIDS

Process	1	2	3	4	5
Quality function deployment					
CORE					

Figure 3.1. Outline of quality practices for inclusion in the quality plan. (*Continues.*)

TOOLS

Tool	1	2	3	4	5
Automatic code checker					
Random test case generator					

QUALITY INITIATIVES

Initiative	1	2	3	4	5
Ignoring for at least 48 hours any requirements received immediately after the CEO has been to lunch with the customer					

Figure 3.1.   Outline of quality practices for inclusion in the quality plan. (*Concluded.*)

Table 3.2.   Quality measurement matrix

	Cap'y	Use'y	Perf	Rel'y	Instl'y	Maint'y	Doc'n
Customer view	×	×	×	×	×	×	×
Postprocess	×	×	×	×	×	×	×
Inprocess	×	×	×	×	×	×	×

Table 3.3.   Reliability targets

	Projection	Predecessor
User defects/KLOC	$x.x$	$x.x$
Problems/user month	$x.xxx$	$x.xxx$
MTTF	$xx.xx$ (days)	$xx.xx$ (days)

x per cent improvement on the previous release. Our projections are as shown in Table 3.3. This data will be captured as follows:

- User defects per thousand lines of source code—defects from user error reports assessed as defining valid defects; defects per thousand lines of source code from the final sizings given by the program library administrator package.
- Problems/user month—problems as reported by the user error reports, whether identifying valid defects or not; dates from the service department as part of their logging process.

- MTTF—calculated and reported by the user in consultation with the service engineer and the project office.

Postprocess reliability measures

As for customer view reliability measures. No additional measures are deemed necessary.

Inprocess reliability measures

Product X will maintain a defect removal model (DRM) for tracking reliability within the development process. (See Sec. 3.6 for a detailed explanation of defect removal models). The initial version of our model is shown in Fig. 3.2. It will be updated as actual data becomes available.

	Defects brought forward	Defects added	Total defects	Removal efficiency %	Defects out	Defects left	Fix inject rate
	Calc	Est	Calc	Est	Calc	Calc	Est
Code section 1 (9.05 KLOC)							
Predesign	0.00	10.00	10.00	60.00	6.00	4.00	
Design/code	4.00	34.00	38.00	60.00	22.80	15.20	
Unit test	15.20	1.23	16.43	60.00	9.86	6.57	0.13
Build ver'n	6.57	0.04	6.61	5.00	0.33	6.28	0.13
FV test	6.28	0.60	6.89	70.00	4.82	2.07	0.13
Code section 2 (4.64 KLOC)							
Predesign	0.00	10.00	10.00	60.00	6.00	4.00	
HLD	4.00	15.00	19.00	60.00	11.40	7.60	
LLD	7.60	18.00	25.60	60.00	15.36	10.24	
Code	10.24	20.00	30.24	60.00	18.14	12.10	
Unit test	12.10	0.98	13.08	60.00	7.85	5.23	0.13
Build vers'n	5.23	0.03	5.26	5.00	0.26	5.00	0.13
FV test	5.00	0.48	5.48	70.00	3.84	1.64	0.13
Code ported (262.00 KLOC)							
Build ver'n	0.82	0.01	0.83	5.00	0.04	0.78	0.13
FV test	0.78	0.01	0.79	10.00	0.08	0.71	0.13
System test (13.69 New/Changed α 262.00 Ported KLOC)							
New & chg	1.84	0.16	2.01	65.00	1.31	0.70	0.13
Ported	0.71	0.01	0.72	10.00	0.07	0.65	0.13
Total product						0.66	

Figure 3.2. Example of 'complex' defect removal model.

Defect data will be captured as follows:

- Design/code phases—valid defects found during inspections; these will be recorded online using the LINEITEM tool.
- Unit test—valid defects reported by programmer's unit test logs; these will not be recorded online.
- FV, system test—valid defects reported by the respective test groups; these will be recorded online using the integrated development support system tool.

If the quality plan is generated in this form, then measurements will be thought about and determined at the right time—at the beginning of development, rather than when somebody thinks that things seem not to be going too well, so perhaps we should start measuring.

If treated as a 'living document', as opposed to a 'once-for-all, thank- goodness-that's-done, stick-it-on-the-shelf-quick' plan, then it will serve the useful purpose of maintaining the right level of focus on quality throughout—and beyond—development.

3.6   Case study: defect removal modelling

Producing defect-free software is not about producing software without making a single error throughout the development cycle, it is about—and this is quite different—delivering defect-free software to the customer. The reality is that defects will occur and, so long as those defects are found before the product reaches the customer, their generation in some limited number is acceptable.

This begs a few questions, of course, the biggest of which is: what is an 'acceptable' defect level for any stage of development (including use by the customer, which is the overall development objective)? Is the finding of large numbers of defects an indicator of highly efficient testing and, thus, of high quality software, or is it an indication that many defects have been found because many exist, and that the software is of appalling quality?

The defect removal model (DRM) is used extensively within IBM as a mechanism for assessing—that is, for measuring—defect levels throughout the development cycle. It is based on the simple concept of *defect density*—the number of defects in a standard sized piece of code (a thousand lines of code, or KLOC). It is a *measure* because it is a direct *quantification* of that concept. This is a useful concept for the development team, because it gives some idea of the relative freedom (or otherwise) of errors for a piece of code, and it is defensible provided LOC are counted in a standard repeatable way (using a tool) and there are agreed-upon definitions of defects in place.

Thus defect density is a good metric (according to the criteria in the first part of this chapter). The DRM extends its usefulness with the concept of *defect removal patterns*. This concept is that a 'good' development cycle will remove defects in a well-established pattern, and that any deviation from that pattern is a cause for concern. The DRM models that pattern, and is used for tracking deviations.

	Defects brought forward	Defects added	Total defects	Removal efficiency %	Defects out	Defects left	Fix inject rate
	Calc	Est	Calc	Est	Calc	Calc	Est
Predesign	0.00	9.00	9.00	60.00	5.40	3.60	
Design	3.60	18.00	21.60	55.00	11.88	9.72	
Code	9.72	9.00	18.72	20.00	3.74	14.98	
Unit test	14.98	1.87	16.85	35.00	5.90	10.95	0.13
FV test	10.95	1.37	12.32	85.00	10.47	1.85	0.13
System test	1.85	0.23	2.08	65.00	1.35	0.73	0.13
Total product						0.73	

Figure 3.3.   Example of 'simple' defect removal model.

In its basic form, a DRM consists of nothing more than a simple two-dimensional matrix such as that shown in Fig. 3.3. Each row of the model should be thought of as representing a defect removal activity, and not simply as a development or testing phase. In this way the model maintains its relevance whatever the actual development process (waterfall, incremental design, rapid prototyping, or whatever) used. The columns of the matrix reflect the extent (in terms of defects/thousand lines of code—defects/KLOC) to which defects are removed, or not, by each activity:

- *Defects brought forward*   Defects not found by the previous activity. Note that the predesign phase need not always be zero! A follow-up release of an existing product would 'bring forward' the earlier release's final 'defects left' value.
- *Defects added*   An estimate of the number of new defects added by development, and that this defect-removal activity could potentially discover.
- *Total defects*   Sum of the previous two elements.
- *Removal efficiency*   An estimate of the percentage of defects that this activity will actually remove.
- *Defects out*   For the removal efficiency, a computation of actual numbers of defects that will be removed per KLOC.
- *Defects left*   The number of defects/KLOC not found by the removal activity, and which therefore pass 'forward' to the next removal activity or—the bottom line—the actual number of defects/KLOC remaining in the final product.
- *Fix inject rate*   A feedback value, for the test phases, reflecting the number of defects introduced in fixing other defects! The value in the example represents one new defect for every eight fixed.

In summary: defects are brought forward from the previous removal activity; augmented by further defects generated by new development work; and a proportion subsequently removed, according to some removal efficiency figure, to give estimates both of defects resolved by the activity and of defects which survive to pass on to the subsequent removal activity.

This simple modelling technique is highly effective. It is trivial to implement—any sixpenny spreadsheet package can do the trick—and concise. It provides, in its first incarnation, targets against which progress can be measured. Later versions can be produced as actual defect numbers become known, and the model gradually refined.

A constant need, however, is to ensure continually that the model is accurately reflecting the defect-removal activity that is actually taking place. The simple model shown, for instance, would be adequate for a development comprising entirely new code. It would not be an adequate model with the common 'later release' development, where only part of the code is being produced from scratch with the bulk being ported from a previous release. Similarly, and for valid (or invalid) reasons, different sections of code might be subjected to different levels of defect removal activity. An enhancement of the simple model would be necessary here also. Thus the simple model of Fig. 3.2 will invariably be extended into a more complex form shown (as a set of hypothetical figures) in Fig. 3.1.

Here we have a block of code (Code section 1) which is receiving 'accelerated' defect-removal attention—perhaps because it is simple or well understood. A second block (Code section 2) is receiving exhaustive attention. A third section, of ported code, is only being subjected to defect removal activity from build verification onwards.

The model reflects this situation by having two different new/changed code sections and a ported code section. They each generate a 'defects left' value (2.07, 1.64, 0.71 defects/KLOC respectively) following the completion of functional verification testing. These values are combined into a weighted average 'defects brought forward' value (of 1.84) to take into the system test phase. Similarly the bottom line value of 0.66 defects/KLOC remaining is derived from computing the weighted average of the new/changed and ported sections of code, i.e.

$$\text{Total product} = \frac{(13.69 \times 0.70) + (262.00 \times 0.65)}{13.69 + 262.00}$$

3.6.1   The DRM as a predictive tool

Simple as it is, a DRM can deliver information which is of considerable use to a project manager. 'Defects out' figures, for instance, provide estimates of what the inspection and test phases can be expected to achieve. The bottom line value for 'defects remaining in the product' can be used in estimating the amount of 'bug-fixing' support activity that will be needed in the period after the product has been shipped. This enables various assessments to be made:

- How much effort will be involved in finding the expected number of defects? (Bearing in mind that the model refers to valid defects only, and that to this

figure has to be added the invalid defect reports which are an inevitable by-product of the testing process.)
- For a fixed level of resource, how long will any particular testing phase have to last in order that the required number of defects be found?
- Given the defects/KLOC remaining in the product, what level of service activity needs to be catered for?

In addition, the outputs from the model provide a yardstick by which likely code quality can be assessed. The argument is that an acceptable matching of predicted defects against actual defects for any development phase is a useful indicator that the developed product is on track to meet its code quality goals. Any particular phase which proves to be deficient in the number of defects found should trigger an investigation, since it may mean that corrective action of some form will be needed. This need not be the case, of course. A good design by an experienced team might be expected to achieve a reduction in detected inspection errors as compared to levels achieved by previous products. The important thing is that deviation from the model is taken as a warning of potential trouble and that the reasons for the deviation need to be understood. If the deviation is not indicative of goodness, appropriate corrective action may then be taken.

For instance, should fewer defects than anticipated have been found during the high-level design phase then some of the options to consider could include:

- Additional design reviews
- Revised plans for additional testing (with all the schedule implications which that holds)
- Acceptance (perish the thought!) of a higher number of defects left on the bottom line

At the end of the project, a comparison of the numbers of defects actually found against the numbers predicted by the model will suggest those phases of the process which were delinquent and which should be improved next time round.

The astute reader will have spotted a certain amount of chicken-and-eggedness about what has been presented so far. The outputs from a DRM depend on the 'inputs'—for each phase, estimates of how many defects will be added, and how efficiently they will be removed. But where do these estimates come from? The answer, of course, is from previously successful DRMs. Generating the primeval DRM is something of a problem, therefore. In the absence of any information from previous projects, estimates of defect removal efficiencies and errors added are going to be highly dependent on which way the wind is blowing.

But what if data is available? Even then, the DRM 'inputs' are going to be estimates and nothing more. Products, even follow-on releases of a product, are not necessarily going to follow the same development pattern as their predecessors. Even though the development process might be the same, the developers might not.

Consider some of the factors that might increase/decrease the DRM 'defects added' estimate during the code phase:

- Experience of coder
- Coder's familiarity with programming language
- Programming language being used
- Program development tools being used

Similarly, factors affecting the 'defect removal efficiency' for a design phase might include:

- Number of review meetings
- Experience of reviewers
- Experience of designers
- Design tools being used

Practical point number one, therefore, is that a DRM is not a precision instrument (in spite of the fact that it uses numbers to two places of decimals) but a tool which provides information from which assessments can be made and corrective actions triggered. The base assumption here is that the model is an accurate reflection of what is actually happening—which brings us to practical point number two.

It is a mistake to regard a DRM as static. The initial model, generated as part of the product's quality plan, has to be regarded as just that—an initial model, an estimate based on past experience. As the development process proceeds, and actual figures become available, the DRM must be refined in the light of investigations into why any deviations have occurred. Deviations may be signs of goodness or badness; what is important is that the DRM reflects them.

Part Two
CORE—Creating the optimum risk environment

There are two facets to creating the optimum risk environment (CORE):

- Anticipating risk
- Planning for risk

The problem that the risk manager has to cope with is that the risks are to a large extent derived from the characteristics of the product being developed. For instance, it may have stringent performance requirements, it may need to run on a target machine that has not yet reached the field, it may need to be ultrareliable because of potentially life-threatening situations, and so on.

As we have already seen, risks are not real until you have a commitment, and the commitments are made in the product's objectives, when quantitative values are put on each characteristic; but these can only be derived from a good understanding of the overall requirements of the product. It is for this reason that the general chapters on anticipating and planning for risk are presented here together with specific chapters on defining requirements, and turning them into objectives. Risk management at this stage involves maintaining the risk management plan (RMP) in parallel with the developing appreciation of the demands of the product: there will almost certainly be a degree of interaction (feedback) between the product objectives and the RMP.

The requirements and objectives stages are contiguous with the development stages, of course, so that is the way they have been presented in this book. Figure P2.1 shows the relationship between the chapters in this part. Remember that the establishment of the CORE is essentially iterative, and it becomes better and better defined as the objectives are better defined.

The nature of the management changes significantly through the cycle, for the following reasons:

- The early stages of the software cycle (those covered by this part) require a more creative, free-thinking approach, while the later stages (those covered by Part Three, MORE) require a more logical, precise approach.

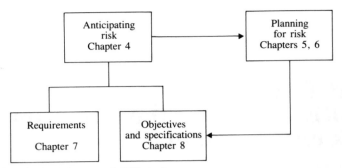

Figure P2.1.   Overview of CORE chapters.

- The early stages tend to be small in volume (of deliverables); the volume of output, and hence resources required, increase enormously through the cycle.

(Some of these ideas are expanded in Chapter 10, 'Verification'.)

What this means in practice is that different thinking approaches are required. In the MORE stages, relatively familiar management techniques are required that most managers will feel comfortable with: measurement, tracking, control. It is in the stages dealt with here that the management techniques are not so obvious, because they are more qualitative in nature. This does *not* mean that they are correspondingly less important. In fact, precisely the opposite is true.

Any misdefinition in the early stages that is undetected will result in the proliferation of work developing function that is wrong. Hence, there is tremendous leverage exerted by the early work on the later stages—get it right, and the project (all the way through to user acceptance) should be relatively trouble-free; get it wrong, and expect trouble—especially when the product reaches the user community.

4
Anticipating risk

The first step in the creation of an optimum risk environment is that of identification. 'Know your enemy' is an appropriate summary of the rationale, even though, as our use of the term 'optimum' implies, risks should not always be regarded as wholly unwelcome. Risks can be accepted, if not exactly with open arms, at least with open eyes. But, and this is the key point, only if those risks are known; if they have been identified and assessed as to their potential impact. Rather like the sentry on the gate, we have enough work to do discovering whether we are dealing with a friend or a foe.

All analogies break down sooner or later, of course, and this one falls into the sooner category. Risks, real risks, tend not to simper delicately into view and call 'coo-ee!' Given the chance, they are far more likely to creep up while you are not looking, then whack you with a sandbag. Risk identification, then, is proactive. It is about taking positive steps to identify risks before they identify you. When a risk manifests itself, it is too late. You are not dealing with risk any more, you are dealing with a crisis.

So, we need to set about identifying potential risks to our project. But at what stage? The standard approach is to conduct a risk identification exercise at preset times, for example:

- Monthly (or even weekly)—as part of a project review cycle
- At major checkpoints

While these might do part of the job, the chances are that some risks will slip through unidentified. Regular meetings will inevitably focus on status and will therefore tend to confirm risks that have matured rather than to spot those at the putative stage.

What we are after here is an approach that sees risk identification as integral to the different stages of whatever development process is being used. That is, risk identification should be part of:

- The planning process
- The development process

- The test process
- The customer involvement process . . .

Risk identification, then, is an essential part of every development activity.

Let us go a step further. We saw in Chapter 1 that the indicator of a risk that has matured is the failure to meet some sort of commitment. That commitment may be in the form of:

- A schedule commitment—'It will be in the post by the end of the day.'
- A financial commitment—'If you see the same product advertised cheaper elsewhere, we will refund the difference.'
- A product/quality commitment—'This product is completely user friendly . . . you will be up and running minutes after unpacking the box.'

The commitment may be to an external (paying) customer or to an internal customer. It makes no difference. A commitment should imply that all necessary risks have been assessed; a failure to meet a commitment is an admission that the risks have won.

Risk identification, then, should be carried out *whenever a commitment is made*. This precept actually encapsulates all of the above, since every step of the planning process effectively amounts to a commitment to produce the deliverables upon which the next step of the process depends.

Is there no place, then, for the weekly/monthly risk review? Far from it. For one thing it is vital that regular reviews be carried out to ensure the effectiveness of actions being taken to address risks, that is, regular reviews are part of the activity of maintaining an optimum risk environment. Through so doing, related risks will often be identified.

These two approaches—commitment driven and periodic—are complementary and both should have a place in a risk management strategy.

The rest of this chapter is organized as follows:

- Identifying risks—methods of generating lists of risks to which your project will be susceptible
- Assessing risks—methods of assessing the severity, or impact, of the risks

4.1   Identifying risks

4.1.1   *Thinking about risk*

The immediate challenge is to identify all possible areas of risk. Simply put, it is to answer the question: what could conceivably go wrong with this project? (A question that some project managers are tempted to ask only rhetorically, because that way, they are more likely to hear the answer 'nothing'!)

As with any exercise in information-gathering, there are a number of sources:

Common sense

Also known as 'gut-feel'. Let us get this one out of the way first. Instinct for what 'does not feel right' is as valid, and valuable, a risk identification technique as any of those that follow. We are not robots. If nothing else, instinct about the possible source of a risk will lead to an investigation of that area. Our fears may then prove to be unfounded or they may not. Pursuing gut-feel is quite different from flying by the seat of one's pants. A much more reliable part of the anatomy is involved.

Past experience

We learn from our mistakes, goes the saying. Possibly. The regular arrival of computing horror stories might call the saying into question. Even so, what we actually mean is that we learn from our bad experiences. If they count for anything, they should count as a source of risks that were not identified soon enough.

Because our own memories are notoriously short with respect to our own mistakes, try thinking of mistakes that others have made. And, while you are at it, ask them to think of yours. (Learning from the optimum risk environment (LORE), in other words, a topic covered in Part Four.)

Historical data/database

Project data, if it exists, is invaluable. Ideally it should include a complete set of plans and actuals, with commentary on any gap between the two. The chances are that it will not be complete. Even so, it will be a valuable source of information. It is usual that the plans made in the enthusiasm of project startup exist, while the documentation of what actually happened does not, such unproductive stuff having been abandoned in the panic of meeting an eroding schedule. Dig those plans out, and ask 'what really happened'?

Tools and aids (e.g. checklists, expert systems)

The value of a standard checklist of risk areas can be overestimated. Like humans, no two projects are identical. However, also like humans, projects have sufficient similarities—arms, legs, design, code—to make a systematic approach such as that of a checklist worth while. It could well be that a starter checklist will fall out of the past experience/creative thinking activities.

Expert systems and other tools for risk identification are pretty thin on the ground. If you find one, it is likely to fall into the category of an automated checklist. The best guide to risk is history.

Use of independent assessors

The rationale for bringing in an outsider is simply that a completely fresh eye may spot something that you—through familiarity—may overlook (or, through that reluctance we all have about admitting our own shortcomings, may want to overlook). This can be an expensive option; it can also be less effective than one might think. Remember that your independent consultant may be one of those who did not survive the risk learning curve in their own projects!

An alternative is to use another part of your own organization to carry out an assessment, either from square one, or of the risks that you have identified.

Analogues

There is another way of 'going outside' that should not be overlooked, namely, that of examining the approach taken to risk by completely different industries. Looking at the sort of risks that the motor insurance industry deals with, for instance, is the most obvious. Trying the less obvious might also be worth while. Looking at how a bookmaker handles the risk of losing money can tell you an awful lot about hedging bets!

Creative thinking

Finally, consider innovation. Every one of the sources listed is in some way a method of identifying risks from experience. They will serve us well, but are unlikely to spot the sort of risks which historians like to describe as 'unprecedented'.

Innovation is about leaving aside convention and asking, possibly stupid, what-if questions. That is, not simply asking 'what if my code sizings are too low?', which might lead to the identification of some fairly conventional development risks, but also daring to think the unthinkable. For instance, an exploration of the question 'what if our database guru left the company six months from now?' could uncover some dramatic risks in the area of staffing.

4.1.2   Identification through risk categories

The approaches described previously are essentially to do with gathering information. The result of applying them to the subject of software development risks will result in a 'starter set' of risk areas for the project under review, which it is useful to categorize in some way. This categorization can be handled in what might be termed a 'top-down' or a 'bottom-up' manner. The former views the risks as they relate to the overall development process, the latter as they relate to individual characteristics of that process. Thus a top-down categorization of risks might result in the following hit-list of queries:

- Business risk
  —The market for the product is not as expected.
  —The product cannot be brought to the market in time to capitalize on demand.
  —The product cannot be developed to a price that the customer is prepared to pay.
  —The resources needed—people, equipment, infrastructure—are beyond our capacity.
  —Competitors are already further advanced.
- User acceptance risk
  —The function the customer requires cannot be delivered.
  —A demand for the function in the product cannot be created.
  —The requirements may not have been established correctly.
  —The customers want more than can be delivered.
- Technical risk
  —The required function is beyond current technological capability.
  —The required quality—performance, usability, etc., is beyond current technological capability.
  —There are dependencies on corequisite product ship dates.
  —All external standards may not be met.
- Implementation risk
  —There are not the required skills/abilities to do the job.
  —The most appropriate tools, methods, etc., are not available.
  —The people do not understand the process/there is not enough support to implement the process properly.
  —Ditto with regard to the programming language to be used, development tools, etc.
  —Adequate project management skills are not available.
- External risk
  —The product is dependent on the successful development of another product/component.
  —Some of the work needs to be subcontracted to a third-party developer.
  —A third-party developer cannot deliver on time.
  —Deliverables required by a third-party developer cannot be delivered to them on time.

Alternatively, a bottom-up grouping of risks at the 'component' level might produce similar risks from asking the following questions:

- *Schedule* Will target dates be met for each development phase? For producing deliverables needed by another organization, either internal or external? For announcing the product that we eventually want to ship?

- *Function*   Can we deliver all committed line items? Will they satisfy targets with respect to usability? performance? reliability? maintainability? Will the documentation be complete?
- *Quality*   Can we assess our code quality? Is it satisfactory? What are our expectations for defects remaining in the shipped product?
- *Process*   Do we have plans? Are they valid? Are we tracking to them? Is the development process defined, and is it being followed?
- *Business*   Is the business case for our product still valid? Are we tracking to budget? What are the competition doing—are our prices likely to be under-cut?
- *Resource*   Do we have enough people? Do they have the right skills? Can we give them the equipment they need? Pay them enough? What is the expected attrition rate during the development of our product and is it going to cause problems?
- *Third parties/vendors*   Are we using a vendor when we should not? Not using one when we should? Are our vendor management procedures adequate? How confident are we that we will get deliverables on time? Are they crucial to the successful development of the product?
- *Dependencies*   Is there anything that our product is dependent on from another organization? Are our requirements understood? Is the other organization tracking to schedule? Do we have an organization in place to manage these dependencies?
- *Constraints*   Are there any factors which are totally beyond our control? Might global standards change to which our product must adhere? Are there inextricable links of our ship/announcement dates to those of another, higher priority product?

We tend to favour the second (bottom-up) approach, because it is more commitment driven. It is usually obvious from most of the headings what the relevant project commitment is, and hence the starting point for risk identification. Accordingly, we have used it (in our risk-factor tables) in later chapters.

4.2   Assessing risks

4.2.1   *Factorizing risk*

Risk, as we defined it in Chapter 1, is about the potential for an undesirable outcome. If we refer to the risk involved in crossing the road, for instance, what we are really talking about is the potential for the undesirable outcome of our not reaching the other side in one piece. This definition highlights the two factors which need to be addressed in the assessment of any risk:

- Potential or *likelihood*   What is the probability that the unsatisfactory outcome will actually transpire? The likelihood of being hit by a lorry is presumably lower if we are trying to cross a country road at 3 p.m. than if we are dicing with the rush-hour traffic at 9 a.m. (This illustration presupposes, of course, that the traffic is actually moving as designed.)

- Undesirable outcome or *loss*   If the risk materializes, what will be the cost to us, either in financial terms or in some other unit of measure? If we fail to cross the road, is the expectation that it will cost us our life or merely an arm and a leg?

These two factors, when taken together, give an indication of the *severity* of any risk—an important concept, about which more will be said later.

Suffice to say at this point that both likelihood and loss need to be quantifiable in some meaningful way. The reasons for this should be self-evident. If neither can be quantified, how can any risk be assessed? And if it cannot be assessed, how can proposed actions to deal with that risk be assessed, and their actual effectiveness (or lack of it) be determined? Having said that, however, it must also be said that an open mind must be maintained about what can, and cannot, be used as a valid measure.

The ability to produce a value that is correct to 14 places of decimals is not necessarily what we are looking for. The criteria for a decent measure are that:

- It is finite.
- It is consistent.
- It is capable of meaningful manipulation.

(and also that it actually measures something useful—it is very easy to get seduced into measuring something simply because it is easy to measure, rather than it telling you what you need to know).

This said, we now look at the possibility of measuring the two component parts of any risk: likelihood and loss.

Likelihood

Ask a police officer about the likelihood of crossing the road safely and you would not expect to be told 'Nought point one four three'. What you would expect to get, along with a considerable amount of teeth-sucking, would be something along the lines of 'highly unlikely'. Ask about crossing a country lane safely, and the response might be 'very likely', or maybe even 'absolutely certain, so long as you wait there until I have stopped all the traffic'.

Words are regularly used to represent likelihood. So why not use them as a springboard for generating numbers? By allowing the use of a very limited lexicon of terms for describing likelihood, a simple mechanism such as that shown in Fig. 4.1 could be used to convert any word into a numerical equivalent.

Now one could argue at length about the finer semantic points of this chart. That would be to miss its purpose, which is to give us a reference point for

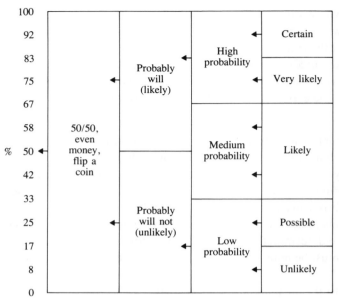

Figure 4.1.   Word-to-probability relationships.

common terms about the probability of risk. Risk assessments need to be communicated. In order to do so without ambiguity, a common understanding has to exist about the 'size' connotations attached to terms expressing likelihood. This is what the chart seeks to do.

The scale on the y-axis is shown in terms of percentages. It could equally well show a scale running from 0 to 1—which would suggest a probability range from impossible to certain—or a 'marks out of ten' scale of 0 to 10. In some ways the last is preferable to either of the preceding two. Risk, especially software risk, is not very susceptible to precise quantification. In fact, attempting to do so is almost counterproductive. Suggesting that there is a 43.26 per cent risk of X is to imply a level of analytical accuracy that simply cannot be justified.

The latest fashion in weather forecasting is an example. We now hear statements like: 'there is a 60 per cent chance of rain in Portsmouth today'. Ignoring the question of whether such a prediction means anything at all (will 60 per cent of the city get wet, all of it get 60 per cent wet, etc?), the sheer fact that a number is quoted is to suggest that weather forecasting is a precise science, when one only has to get caught in a 100 per cent hurricane to realize that it certainly is not.

Loss

Likelihood may be difficult to compute, but at least it is a clear concept: a probability is a probability. Loss is much harder to deal with. The problem is that losses are not always comparable. Two losses may differ in their *nature*, and they may differ in their *extent*. Even with losses of the same nature, a straightforward comparison may not always be possible.

The following examples should illustrate the problems:

- A financial loss—of capital, revenue, or both—is relatively simple, being measurable in terms of some quantity of pounds, dollars, yen, or whatever. The extent of the loss is a total value to be sure, but that loss may be instantaneous or it may be eked out over a period of time. The difference could be critical, with one loss being survivable, the other not.

- A time loss, that is, schedule delay. The unit is measure is obviously that of time, with the extent of loss being computed in terms of days, months, and/or years. But is time really the same as money?

- A loss of functionality, that is, of some property that the product should possess. We could extend this notion to include not only executable function but also such aspects as usability, performance, etc. The unit of measure becomes—what? The best that can be done may be to split out the different elements and come up with measures for each: performance in terms of response time, perhaps, and usability in terms of time-to-learn or number-of-questions-asked.

- A loss of quality—one or more of the above, or some other criterion? Fewer defects removed than anticipated, for instance? Now the unit of measure is becoming a lot harder to pin down. What would be the extent of the loss in quality if the Mona Lisa had a blob of Plasticine placed on the end of her nose? The difficulty of defining quality might mean that we end up with a multitude of measures—for elements such as usability, performance, maintainability, etc.—or that we settle for a lowest common denominator, such as counting the ubiquitous, and open-to-many-interpretations, 'defect'.

- A loss of resource (people, skills, equipment), leading to losses across all areas. Money is the obvious unit of measure, but quantification is likely to be a headache. Replacement costs may be easy to compute, but how about costs of nonreplacement?

- A loss of reputation—intangible, but nevertheless very real. How is this to be measured, and in what units? Number of customers lost? Number of orders not received? Drop in CEO's invitations to Buckingham Palace?

The list could be extended, of course. Loss of life with safety-critical systems, loss of integrity with banking systems, loss of data with real-time systems—all might be classified as different types of loss, with different units of measure. The question, therefore, is not: are we comparing like with like? Clearly we are not, and yet compare them we must. The question becomes, then: how do we compare chalk with cheese?

One way is to develop a common currency for the quantification of any loss. In the foregoing discussion, two units of measure may well have suggested themselves to you:

- Time
- Money

Can any form of loss—even an intangible such as loss of reputation—be reduced to one or the other? There are plenty of examples to suggest that they can.

In 1990, the Perrier water-bottling company discovered that their source was contaminated with benzene in microscopic quantities. Immediately, they withdrew all supplies: bottles were removed from supermarket shelves, returned to the factory, and destroyed. The bottling plant was closed down, and thoroughly re-engineered to remove the source of the contamination. At the same time, a massive advertising campaign kept the public informed of what was going on. Eventually, in a blaze of publicity, the plant re-opened, and sales rapidly regained their former level. It is likely that the Perrier company knows *exactly* how much each of these measures cost them: the cost of restoring a reputation that nose-dived can be calculated to the last penny.

Ultimately, circumstances will determine what is possible in this direction and what is not. Examples that we use in this book do reduce loss to either time or money (or both) in every case.

4.2.2   *Risk assessment considerations*

Uncertainty

Using a common currency will not resolve all of the problems of assessment, however. In fact, what a clear comparison will inevitably highlight is that—for both likelihood and loss—we are faced with another factor to be taken into account, that of uncertainty.

Students of applied mathematics will know that it is common practice to cut one's teeth on problems which ignore tricky, real-world influences such as friction. The principle is that, although by so doing the problems (and the answers) can never be absolutely accurate, they do at least bear a close resemblance to realism. In other words, the element of uncertainty introduced by ignoring friction is not so great as to totally distort the situation.

We need to establish the same level of confidence when dealing with uncertainty in our risk assessments. This is not easy. Estimates of likelihood and/or loss can quite regularly descend to the level of 'sorry, have not got a clue'. In such cases we have to appreciate that our primary risk is that of not knowing how great the risks are.

The solution then is not to start thinking of ways of dealing with the risks that we have identified—because if they cannot be assessed how do we know they are risks at all?—but of ways of reducing our level of uncertainty. The extent to which this can be achieved will influence the accuracy with which it is possible to estimate the severity level of any risk.

Risk severity

Risk severity is an indicator of the degree of the risk being faced. By calculating this severity, risks can be compared—and thus prioritized. In an ideal world all risks would be reduced to zero, but nobody in their right mind has ever claimed that software development takes place in an ideal world. Realistically, we aim to address the risks that matter. That can only be achieved through an exercise of comparison and, thereby, prioritization.

The difficulty, as we have seen, is that both likelihood and loss are terms that can only be computed with uncertainty—sometimes considerable uncertainty. Where uncertainty is great, that becomes the risk that we must seek to minimize. An important first step towards achieving this is that of not asking too much of our method of computing risk severity. If our estimates of likelihood are, at best, ballpark figures, and our measures of cost ill defined (or, more likely, incompatible for our identified risk areas), then the method of assessing risk severity must be tempered accordingly.

4.2.3 *Techniques for risk severity assessment*

In this section we look at four methods of assessing the risk severities. Each is suited to particular levels of uncertainty.

Yes/no questioning

Towards the extreme of maximum uncertainty we might have very little idea about the quantitative aspects of either likelihood or loss. All we might be able to say is that some situations, or some proposed actions, are more or less likely—that is, more or less risky—and that we have no real idea about the potential losses associated with each.

The approach in this case is to turn the risk identification checklist into what amounts to a binary questionnaire. Each question has a yes/no answer, nothing more. The key point is that the answer will imply either 'more risk' or 'less risk' for the project. Table 4.1 gives an example.

By working through a detailed checklist such as this, with questions grouped under broad 'primary' risk areas, a pattern of risks and risk severities begins to emerge. A simple bar chart such as that in Fig. 4.2 can then be drawn, with risk areas on the x-axis and risk extent on the y-axis. The individual bars show the proportions of 'increased risk' and 'decreased risk' identified in each area. By arranging the chart in decreasing order of 'more risk' areas, a simple comparison—and hence prioritization—can be made.

Checkbox

This is a technique suitable for situations in which both likelihood and loss can be estimated at a 'yes/no' level in a few major aspects. The result is that aspects which

Table 4.1.   A 'more risk/less risk' checklist: project management

	Less risk	More risk
Are clear project objectives established?	Yes	No
Is there a project manager who is clearly in command of the whole project?	Yes	No
Is there a set of sensible and useful project reviews at appropriate levels?	Yes	No
Do these in practice initiate corrective actions?	Yes	No
Does the project manager have adequate support for project administration?	Yes	No
Is the project manager new to managing projects of this complexity?	No	Yes
Is there a project plan?	Yes	No
Are project managements tools in place and being used?	Yes	No
⋮		

(*Source: IBM Risk Management—Project Risk Assessment Checklist ZU59-801*)

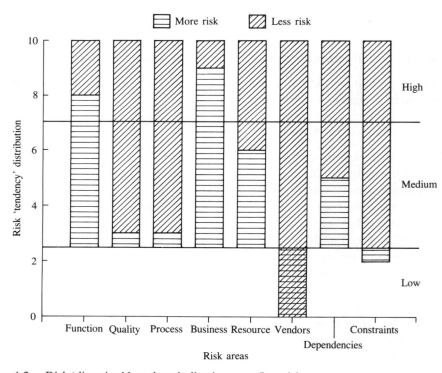

Figure 4.2.   Risk 'direction' bar chart indicating more/less risk.

are both likely and potentially costly are classified as high risk, those which are neither likely nor costly are classified as low risk, and everything in between is classified as medium risk.

The core of the technique is a series of matrices in the form of the example shown in Fig. 4.3, one matrix for each risk area identified. The technique proceeds

Product risk area	Importance				Likelihood						Risk
	1	2	3	Total	4	5	6	7	8	Total	
Function											
Reliability											
Serviceability											
Learnability											
Migratability											
Compatibility											
Installability											
Interfaceability											
Extendability											
Usability											
Performance											
Transparency											
⋮											

Figure 4.3. Checkbox for risk analysis.

as follows. For each identified risk, ask questions 1–8 from the following list. Questions 1–3 are about the importance (i.e. potential loss) associated with the risk, 5–8 about the likelihood of failure. If the answer to any question is 'yes', tick the relevant column, if 'no' then leave the column blank. (Note that not every question may apply literally to every item on the list.)

1 *Customer cost* Is the aspect of great importance to the customer, i.e. the person who will buy and/or use the product under development?
2 *Internal cost* Will failure in this aspect have a high impact on the remainder of the product? For example, it could be highly likely that the test will finish a week late, but schedule buffers could render this irrelevant (low cost). On the other hand, failure to produce draft manuals in time could prevent the test team from starting in a brief window available before the same group has to test some other product (high cost).
3 *Complexity* Is this a complex aspect of the product?
4 *New ground* Does this aspect of the product break new ground?
5 *Product history* Does recent history suggest that this aspect of the product is likely to fail?
6 *Team history* Did the development team do badly on this aspect last time?

Are there any aspects which the team members themselves perceive as being risky?

7 *Gurus* Does the available specialist advice perceive this to be a potential trouble area?

8 *Expectation* Does the product plan suggest a clear and credible idea/plan/model for this aspect?

Complete the matrix as follows. Any aspect which has a tick in column 1, 2, or 3 is important. Highlight the first total (TOT) box. Any aspect which has a tick in 4, 5, 6, 7 or 8 is likely. Highlight the second total box. The outcome is that any aspect which has two highlighted total boxes is taken to be high risk. Any which has only one box highlighted is medium risk. The rest are regarded as low risk.

For example: usability is one aspect of the product. Perhaps the usability team has never worked on a product like this before, so you may suspect that it will do a poor job. Tick column 6. Perhaps the ultimate users of the product are nontechnical people, so usability is very important. Tick column 2. The risk is both likely and important, and is therefore high.

Applying weighting factors

In cases where we can be rather more confident as regards both likelihood and loss the technique illustrated in Table 4.2 can be employed. Two assumptions are made:

1 The risk element under consideration is narrow enough to have a clearly delineated range of possibilities associated with it.
2 The 'cost' against any risk element is roughly comparable to that of any other risk element in terms of its impact within the overall risk area.

The technique effectively establishes a scale for risk likelihood by defining 'scenarios' from which a choice must be made. In Table 4.2 the scale is 1–10, with the three scenarios amounting to a description of high (=10), medium (=6) and low (=1) risk situations. Clearly a finer scale could be produced if further, distinct, scenarios can be defined.

Loss is represented by a weighting factor, a value in the range 1–10 in our example. This factor represents a comparative assessment of the contribution towards overall loss made by the risk element in question. An overall risk level is computed by taking the sum of the products of likelihood and weight for all risk elements. In the example, the likelihood chosen in each row is indicated by '**' in the appropriate box. Thus, in Table 4.2, an overall risk value of 294 out of a possible maximum of 560 has been computed. In percentage terms this amounts to 52.5 per cent. The trick now is to determine whether or not this constitutes a greater risk than is acceptable.

A technique is to compute ranges for low/medium/high overall risks. One way

Table 4.2. Risk model using weighting factors

Elements	Low risk (value = 1)	Medium risk (value = 6)	High risk (value = 10)	Weight (1–10)	Total
Process management	Process exists, all process stages have owners, both are regularly reviewed	Process exists, and has an overall owner**	Little or no formal process	8	48
Process documentation	Complete process documentation and standards, both regularly reviewed**	Individual activities defined; only code and documentation standards followed	Minimal process documentation; few standards followed, if any	5	5
Work planning	Work planned comprehensively, procedures exist for regular reviews of product's work plan**	Basic work planning carried out, updated occasionally	Work is usually planned by individuals, if then	10	10
Work planning data	All work planning data needed to control the project is collected and stored. Procedures for collecting and storing data regularly reviewed**	Work planning data needed to control the project is collected and stored, but its accuracy is open to question	No work planning data is collected	7	7
Change control	Full change control practised on the software product and its sub-components; change control plan reviewed regularly	A process exists for controlling change due to functional enhancements or errors discovered**	Little or no change control practised	7	42
Quality planning	Comprehensive quality plans exist, reviewed regularly	Elements of a quality plan exist, not necessarily organized into, or referenced from, a single document	Quality is not recognized as something that needs to be planned**	8	80
Review and test procedures	Effective defect removal practised throughout development cycle; procedures regularly reviewed	Some defect removal practised throughout the development cycle, though not necessarily repeatable	Defect removal activities concentrated at end of development cycle**	4	40
Defect prevention	A full defect prevention process is in place, and followed	Some analysis of errors is performed with demonstrable improvements to the development process**	Little analysis of errors with no subsequent attempt made to improve the development process	2	12
Quality data	Quality data collected and retained, its accuracy demonstrable. Collection procedures regularly reviewed	Quality data collected and retained, accuracy not demonstrable	No quality data collected**	5	50
			Total		294/560 = 52.5%

61

Table 4.3. Computed reference points for Table 4.2

	All low	Midpoint	All medium	Midpoint	All high
Total	56	140	224	392	560
% of max	10	25	40	60	100

of doing this is to generate a simple table of scores such as Table 4.3. It shows five values: the score that would be obtained for an assessment with all low risk selections; for all medium; for all high; and the pair of midpoints between these values. A set of ranges for risk levels would then result:

Low risk	10–25%
Medium risk	25–60%
High risk	60–100%

indicating that, in the example, the project is at medium risk. Thus an overall risk assessment is obtained together with an indication of those individual areas which are high risk.

This is also a useful technique for consolidating a number of risk areas which, individually, are difficult to equate in terms of their potential loss.

Risk severity contours

Our fourth technique takes the weighting concept one step further and is applicable for risk analysis in those cases where both the likelihood and the loss can be reasonably well estimated. At the centre of the technique is the premise, introduced in the previous technique, that the product of likelihood and loss factors gives a valid estimate of overall risk, that is:

$$\text{Risk severity (RS)} = \text{Likelihood factor} \times \text{Loss factor}$$

We consider this premise shortly. For now, and assuming that the formula is valid, what is needed for both likelihood and loss is a relative value—on a scale of 1–10, say. Where it is not possible to estimate one or both (to what amounts to an accuracy of 0.1) then a range of values can be stated.

An example of the sort of table produced is shown in Table 4.4. Figure 4.4 shows this information plotted as a polar chart on top of the base set of risk contours, RS = 10, 30, and 50. These base contours represent overall risk severities which might be considered as low, medium and high respectively.

Note that it is the product of likelihood and loss which gives a clear indication of risk priorities. Individually, high likelihood factors (such as that for 'no defect prevention processes') do not suggest an overall high risk because the estimated loss associated with that risk is low. Similarly, a high loss factor (such as 'process documentation incomplete') does not come into play if the likelihood of its occurrence is low. The risks that the technique does highlight, and which are often

Table 4.4. Risk severity contours

Identified risk	Likelihood factor	Loss factor	Risk severity
Ineffective process management	3–4	8	24–32
Process documentation incomplete	1	7	7
Work badly planned	5–7	10	50–70
Poor change control	2–5	6	12–30
Quality plan not ready	6	7	42
Review and test procedures not established	5	2–6	10–30
No defect prevention processes	9	1	9
Insufficient quality data being collected	2–7	6	12–42

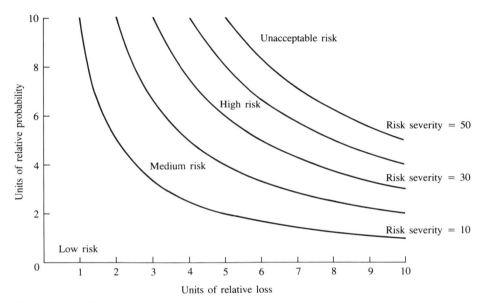

Figure 4.4.   Risk severity contours.

overlooked, are those such as 'quality plan not ready', with average likelihood and loss values but a significant overall severity value of 42.

Caution is needed, of course, in using this approach. It is necessary to be wary of multiplying two pieces of information together to produce a figure which may make an accountant's eyes light up but be of little practical value to a project manager. For instance, the approach would generate the following results:

80% likelihood of £5 loss = 400
60% likelihood of £7 loss = 420
1% likelihood of £500 loss = 500

In numerical terms, each risk is comparable but which would you take out an insurance policy to guard against?

5
Planning how to manage the risks

Chapter 4 discussed the likelihood and cost of a risk materializing. Obviously there are various actions you could take associated with each identified risk, and each of those actions has costs associated with it too, time costs, money costs and maybe quality costs. At the end of the day, time costs can usually be reduced to money costs. The late availability of the product means that the revenue from selling it comes later, so the time slip has cost you a quantifiable amount of money. If you are in a competitive situation, your competitor may even have beaten you to it, causing further financial loss, but that is harder to predict in advance. A loss of quality can also be reduced to a quantifiable loss of money, because you must spend time fixing problems, and a less obvious loss owing to damage to your reputation, which impacts both present and future sales.

It is easy to imagine a situation where so many risks are identified that the cost of putting in preventative action for all of them would more than wipe out any possible benefits from the project. It is even possible to imagine the situation where action taken to prevent risk actually prevents project objectives being met (as in the case of a data collection system that demands so much effort to operate that productivity is significantly reduced).

The obvious course of action is to distinguish between those risks that you have to eliminate and those that you can tolerate with some adjustment, and *plan* what you will do to keep risks at an acceptable level, while maintaining the project activities. This chapter aims to tell you how to optimize your risk environment to suit your own circumstances. It includes:

- The principles of risk planning
- Preparing and documenting the risk management plan (RMP)

5.1   The principles of risk planning

5.1.1   What risks shall we accept?

There are two important things to remember about accepting risk. The first is that everything you choose to do, or choose not to do, involves some degree of risk.

You may not have consciously thought about the risks, but you have—wittingly or unwittingly—accepted risk. The second follows from the observation in Chapter 1 that the degree of risk accepted follows the perceived reward. The corollary is that it is necessary to accept risk to succeed in your enterprise. In a competitive world, the spoils go to those who accept the risks with eyes wide open, and then successfully control them.

The basic risk acceptance precepts are:

- Everything carries some degree of risk, however remote.
- To succeed, some risks have to be understood and accepted.
- The successful risk manager will have quantified those risks that must be controlled, and those that can be lived with.

These precepts are easy enough to write down, but harder to put into practice. There is no magic formula for deciding what actions are appropriate against which risks: we can only point out that risks can be analysed, likelihoods and import-ances discovered, alternative risk management actions proposed, and those actions costed. By thinking things through, you will decide and broadcast your own personal level of acceptable risk.

Reinhold Niebuhr's philosophy seems to sum up the ideal risk manager's attitude: 'God grant me the serenity to accept the things I cannot change, the courage to change the things I can; and the wisdom to know the difference'.

5.1.2 *Managing/influencing risks*

Having analysed and investigated the risk, and decided you cannot accept it, but have to do something about it, what options are open to you? There are only two risk parameters, so there are only two things you could possibly change:

- Likelihood
- Importance/significance

You cannot change the likelihood of an earthquake, except by moving to a country where earthquakes are rarer. You can change how significant it is to you by changing the impact it has on you—possibly by living in a single-storey building with a lightweight roof. Both would be very costly, and you probably reject them and accept the risk, even though the importance to you if the risk materializes is high.

You can change the likelihood of a heart attack, statistically at least, by reducing your intake of fats, and by taking more exercise. But, like a software project, is is difficult to tell your own personal susceptibility to a heart attack compared with your neighbour; and, it is harder to change the impact of a heart attack, except possibly by living next door to a hospital, or by marrying a nurse, so that you receive treatment as soon as possible.

Similarly, you will find with your software risks that you can make some less likely, and you can change the impact which some of them have through contingency planning.

Another dimension to consider is the nature of the risk. In Chapter 1, we identified two ways in which risks are realized:

- Through unknowns (lack of information)
- Operating at the limit of performance

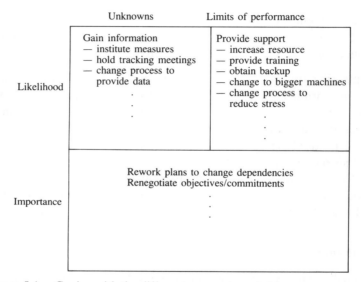

Figure 5.1.   Coping with the different parameters of risk.

If you happen to know that a house is built on a fault line, the risk of the house falling down in an earthquake then becomes a 'limit of performance' risk. If you do not know whether the house is on a fault line or not, the risk then becomes an 'unknowns' type of risk. The ways of coping with the different parameters of risk are summarized in Figure 5.1.

There are three basic kinds of action you can plan to take, in decreasing order of effect:

- Change or avoid
- Control
- Monitor

To illustrate these three actions, consider as an example a project where it is proposed to use four different software vendors to produce four components of a software package, and where one of these components is the control module which holds the other three together.

Imagine first that because of past experiences with vendors in general you regard this as being a high risk situation. There is a strong likelihood that a component will arrive late, because a vendor will be working at the limit of their performance, and the whole product will be unavailable when promised, costing you both revenue and reputation.

You could decide to *change* the plan. You might eliminate the weak link entirely, and persuade another vendor to take on another component, or you could try and perform some of the work in-house. Maybe you could ensure that the control component is given to the most reliable vendor. This action might cost you something, it might well increase the schedule, but would decrease the likelihood of an unacceptable slip to an acceptable level. It will not eliminate the risk entirely, but what your action will have achieved is a reduction of the risk likelihood.

Perhaps you still see a medium risk with this plan. Perhaps one of the vendors has produced code with poor reliability. You might try to *contain* this risk by putting in place a sophisticated tracking mechanism which the vendor could use to report to you on the progress of discovery of defects. That way you could spot quality problems, visit the vendor and instigate corrective actions if the need arose. You could even have prepared a contingency plan, which you could swing into action as soon as the quality problem was discovered. Again, cost is involved, the direct cost of implementing the system, also a small indirect cost if the tracking system takes time to install and run.

You might still feel that there is a low risk left with the other vendors and that you should *monitor* what they do. This could involve visits, status meetings and so on, and again would cost money, probably just direct money. The cost would increase with the frequency of the visits.

And there is a fourth course of 'action', which is inaction. Do nothing. This itself has associated costs, the costs of the basic risk materializing, so it is with this that you can compare the cost of the alternative actions you might wish to take and determine whether it makes sense to take them or not.

To summarize the approaches to managing different degrees of risk:

High risk   Change the risk, through planning. Plan to change:

- Likelihood
- Importance

Medium risk   Contain the risk, by being ready to take action as soon as your tracking mechanism indicates.

Low risk   Monitor that the risk level has not increased.

5.1.3   *Strategy for addressing risk*

The ideas from the previous section can be folded into the risk-factor table approach advocated in Chapters 1 and 4.

1   Go through each of the tertiary factors, identifying if:

   (a)   People or things will be exercised at the limit of their performance: mark them with an 'L' for 'limiting'.

   (b)   There are significant unknowns associated with the factor: mark them with an 'X' for 'unknowns'

2   For each X or L identify a change or action to address the risk:

   (a)   For the Ls, improve support: provide tools, training, etc.

   (b)   For the Xs, identify the missing information, and plan for how and when you can get it.

3   Reassess the risk against each tertiary.

4   For each of the secondary factors, assess the contribution of the X/L tertiaries, and categorize each secondary as:

   (a)   'C' for 'comfortable' about the risk.

   (b)   'U' for 'uncomfortable' about the risk.

5   For each U factor, think creatively about a new approach that minimizes or replaces the risky tertiaries, and reassess.

6   For each of the primary factors, assess the contribution of the U/C secondaries, and categorize each primary as:

   (a)   'C' for 'comfortable' about the risk.

   (b)   'U' for 'uncomfortable' about the risk.

7   For each U in the primaries, attempt to renegotiate the terms or scope of work of the project.

To summarize the strategy for reducing risk:

- Provide support where performance is being pushed to the limit.
- Identify what information you do not have, and plan to get it.
- Integrate up from low factors to determine level of comfort.
- Rethink approach on secondary factors, if uncomfortable.
- Renegotiate terms on primary factors, if uncomfortable.

5.1.4   Schedule risk

Based on your experience, you may feel that coding a particular module will take 2 weeks. That is an average, and the tolerance seems to be plus or minus 2 days for 95 per cent of modules of a similar size. Are there other factors about this module, other than its size, which can give us a closer estimate? Its complexity? Its interrelationship with other modules? The experience of the coder? We can probably say that it has a zero chance of being finished in one week. Barring World War Three, meteorites, earthquakes, fire and flood, it will almost certainly be finished in three weeks—no similar module has ever taken longer. So, what do you write in the project plan?

If you write three weeks, you will almost certainly finish on time, but if you do this for all the activities, your project will take three years instead of two. In a competitive world, this is unacceptable. If you write one week, you will certainly not finish on time. You will commit to your management that you will take a year on the project, their financial plan will rely on this, you will probably take two years, and blow the company's profit out of the water.

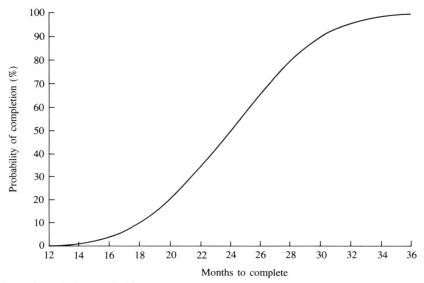

Figure 5.2. Completion probability curve.

A technique we have seen used is to draw an S-shape prediction curve (Fig. 5.2) based on the information we have about every activity. Interpreting this:

- The project has no chance of finishing in less than 12 months.
- It has a 100 per cent probability of finishing within 3 years. Some dire catastrophe would be needed for this to be exceeded.
- The mean finishing time is 24 months, you may like to keep this in your mind as the time you expect the project to take.
- You have an 80 per cent chance of finishing within about 27 months. That is the kind of estimated completion date you might give your management. If the project is average, you will finish 3 months early.
- You have a 20 per cent chance of finishing within 21 months. The 21 month schedule is the one you might like to tell your team you are working to, as a way of encouraging them to keep their heads down.

That is roughly as preached, but the authors are more honest souls and would recommend complete openness both up and down the management chain, presenting a schedule of 24 months with a 60 per cent chance of being up to 3 months either way (or your own version of these numbers). After all, your own business managers probably have some idea of the risk which they and the market are prepared to tolerate, and it will help them if you are as straight as you can be.

5.1.5   *Compounding of risks*

Of course, risks do not necessarily materialize one at a time, and on occasion risks may compound. The total impact of a set of risks may not be the simple sum of the individual risks. To take a trivial domestic example: the risk of leaving an upstairs window open while you are out is that the rain may blow in; the risk of leaving a ladder lying on the ground is that someone may trip over it. The risk of the two risks compounded is that a burglar may break into the house—a different order of magnitude entirely.

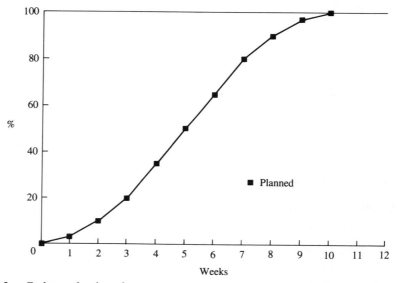

Figure 5.3.   Code production plan.

There are similar examples in software. The one shown here is on the subject of code production.

1 Figure 5.3 shows that the development team plans to develop an amount of code over a 10-week time period, in an S-shape fashion.
2 Figure 5.4 shows actual delivery of code from the developers. It appears that after seven weeks they are about a week behind plan. What do you forecast will happen?

   (a) Will the actual line continue in the S-shape pattern and end up about two weeks late?
   (b) Can they catch up the schedule by putting more people on the coding?

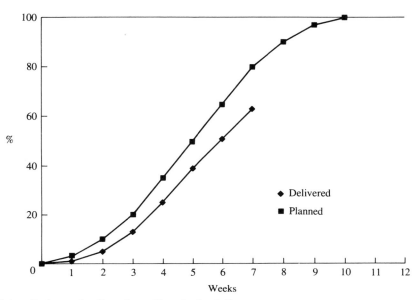

Figure 5.4.   Code production plan with actuals: delivery.

(c)   Are the most difficult programs still to come, so that even more time will be lost from now on, or did the coders tackle the most difficult programs first, so they would be able to make up time later?

How much effort do you put into making the prognosis?

3   Figure 5.5 also shows a third line—how much of the delivered code has been inspected and signed off. We had tacitly assumed that the code delivered was correct, but in fact it had not yet been inspected! There appears to be a heavy overload on people fixing inspection problems. Perhaps the need to fix inspection problems is preventing some coders from developing their new code, which is reflecting in turn on the actuals line. If you draw an imaginary horizontal line back from the right-hand end of the 'signed-off' line, you will see that sign-off is currently about two weeks after delivery, which is in turn one week behind plan. We might prognose that if the same trend continues, code completion will be about six weeks behind plan.

4   And now (Fig. 5.6) the ladder reaches the window sill! It is brought to our attention that the actual number of lines in each model is higher than we had planned for. Every new module which arrives is bigger than expected. After 7 weeks there is already 30 per cent more code than we had planned for. We might forecast that this trend will continue until all the code is delivered. Obviously the key question now is not where the inspected line will meet the 100 per cent line, but where it will meet the actuals line.

That completes our discussion of planning and tracking risks. There follow two templates, one for a risk management strategy and one for a risk management

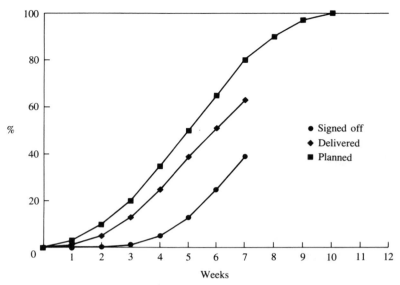

Figure 5.5.   Code production plan with actuals: signed-off.

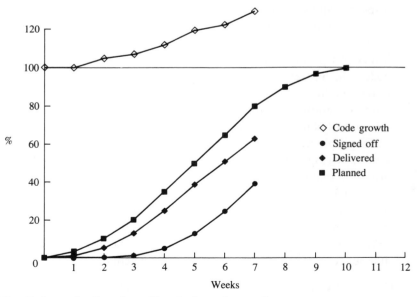

Figure 5.6.   Code production plan with actuals: code growth.

plan, which you may like to use. But the CORE work is not over yet. There are still more things you can do to give yourself a firm foundation, and we go on to talk about those in Chapter 6.

5.2   The risk management plan

5.2.1   Preparing the risk management plan

Because of the importance of the risk management plan (RMP) to the success of the project, it is worth considering:

- Who is the customer for the plan?
- Who writes the plan?
- Who tracks against the plan?

The customer for the plan is the person who has the responsibility for making the software product, and who is concerned about managing risks which may prevent that happening. The same person—the product manager—should have both those concerns, and so will be interested in owning the RMP, and in having regular assessments of risks, and revision of the RMP in the light of changed priorities.

What the product manager is likely to require is a plan showing:

- Perceived risks throughout the development life of the product
- Costs and likelihoods
- Priorities of risks as seen today
- Costs of various courses of action which could be taken to manage each risk
- A recommended course of action

This leads to the next question: who should write the plan? In practice, this is bound up with the the last question: who should track against the plan? Except in small projects, this sort of work is usually not done by the product manager. There are two possibilities:

- It can be done by someone in the product manager's reporting line, or
- It can be done by an independent agency (which we will call Assurance).

We have had experience of both possibilities. There are of course pros and cons for both, and we try to summarize them here.

Independent (extraproject) risk assessment

Pros

- Developers can use Assurance as an 'agony aunt' for problems that they do not want to take to their own management or colleagues.
- Assurance can be fearless: their salaries are not determined by the product manager.

- A broad base of expertise is built up by dealing with different projects, leading to more effective risk assessment. (Incidentally this, plus the need for succinct and confident reporting upwards, makes for an excellent training for future managers.)

Cons

- There can be some closing of ranks against the perceived enemy, Assurance, when the going gets tough.
- Assurance can have a credibility problem. To adapt Shaw: 'those who can, do; those who can't, join Assurance'. (The answer here is to make it such an attractive post that the best people will want to join.)
- Assurance does not itself have the clout to take action it recommends. It can only persuade by force of irrefutable argument.

Intraproject risk assessment

Pros

- With proper management support, the developers build their own risk assessment skills.
- The product manager can take action directly.
- There should be properly allocated time to perform the task.

Cons

- Risk assessment can easily be seen as nonproductive, and can be inadequately resourced.
- The job is usually given to an assistant to the product manager, with obvious disadvantages in terms of not wanting to be the bearer of bad tidings.

In an ideal world, the product manager should accept that attention to, and management of, risk is an integral part of the job, along with management of the other product attributes: function, usability, performance, and so on. In practice, the rudeness of the real world all too often intrudes.

Ultimately, whether risk assessment is performed from within the project, or from outside, is a decision that you will have to make based on a knowledge of the characteristics of your own organization. The attitude of the people in it—fostered by the management team—will usually be the deciding factor.

5.2.2 Documenting the RMP

Immediately after being appointed, the product manager should nominate a risk assessor (maybe, of course, nominating him or herself—the rest of this section is addressed directly to the risk assessor). Within a month, the risk assessor should have produced an approved risk management strategy. This is a fairly brief document, probably only a side of A4 paper, indicating the general direction the risk management will take. Rather like the checkpoints in mainline development, the idea of producing a strategy before the plan is to reduce the risk of wasting effort producing the wrong kind of plan. The strategy is especially useful if the first checkpoint is a long way off. A sample risk management strategy appears in Appendix 3.

After the strategy comes the plan, ideally within two months of starting work on the project. A sample template is given in Appendix 4 for producing an RMP. It does *not* tell you how to perform risk assessment, *nor* does it tell you how to evaluate risk. It is best read when you are first asked to produce an RMP and not as a casual reading exercise. It will then take you step by step through the plan preparation process. The time required will depend on the size and complexity of the product being assured. It is difficult to separate acquiring knowledge about the product from producing the plan. The only certainty is that you will need as long as you have—this is a long process to make a firm foundation for the development, and needs to be done well.

Documenting dependency risks

There is one risk area which deserves further explanation, that of risks which are outside your span of control, but within someone else's, where you have an opportunity to talk to them before the risks materialize.

There will be occasions when you can identify risks, but they are outside your sphere of control. The vendor example given earlier is such a situation; other frequent examples are of a product being developed in parallel at two different sites, or where two related but interdependent products are being developed at two sites. Where this is the case, a document of understanding will help to minimize the risk. Documents of understanding are one way of assuring that there has been a meeting of minds on all the important aspects of the relationship between the two areas. There will also be occasions where you have a dependency on another area to supply you with some service: in this case, an SLA is appropriate. See Sec. 2.2.2 for more information on preparing these sorts of plans.

Risk of change

It is a cliché in the software development world that the one unchanging thing is change itself. A common risk that we have observed is that of having a very tight process for a particular stage, but an uncontrolled change control process. The requirements process is a classic example. Often, requirements are deliberated for months before selecting the right ones for the product. Then they are changed at whim using a process which does not have the same controls as the original. Always ensure that the process for changing something is as controlled as the process you used to make it in the first place.

6
Planning how to track the risks

In Chapter 5, we looked at the preparation of the RMP as far as the identification of the risks to be managed. The RMP also needs to specify how the status of all the individual risks is to be consolidated and reported, because in order to manage risk, you need to observe what is happening on a regular basis *and* take appropriate corrective action to bring the project back on track. That is what we cover in this chapter, while later chapters of this book discuss the tracking of particular types of software development risk at different stages.

If you do observe a new risk during the course of a project, you need to adjust your risks list and determine whether or not to act, using the methods described in Chapter 5. The results can be catastrophic if decisive action is not taken when a risk materializes, or if the risk is covered up or ignored. The following example is from an engineering project of a hundred or so years ago.

> John Tasker said that he had been employed in the foundry dressing the columns after they came out of the mould.
> 'What was the biggest hole you filled with Beaumont Egg?'
> 'I cannot say.'
> 'What was its diameter—an inch?'
> 'I cannot say that.'
> 'Give me your idea—tell me.'
> 'We filled up many a hole with Beaumont Egg.'
> 'Where did you get it?'
> 'I made it.'
> 'Of rosin, beeswax, lamp black, and iron borings? Where did you get the money to buy these things?'
> 'Mr Ferguson (leading foreman) gave me the money to buy those things.'
> He had seen hundreds of holes in the iron that was cast, and he had seen them filled by Egg, painted and sent on to the bridge. He had seen a great many more iron columns too faulty to be used, and these had been broken up. How many? He could not say. A hundred, perhaps two hundred.

The words are taken from John Prebble's book *The High Girders* and are an extract from the Board of Trade inquiry into the collapse of the first Tay railway bridge. The bridge opened on 31 May 1878 and collapsed into the Tay on 28 December 1879, as a train crossed it, leading to the loss of 75 lives.

Eventually, software development will finally become a true discipline, as engineering has become today. Meanwhile, it is obvious from the many well-publicized failures in the press that the risks and the defects are seen, patched up and sent out for the customer to find.

In the meantime, this chapter shows:

- How to monitor the risks and report on them
- How to monitor that the project work is being accomplished correctly, and report on that.

6.1 Methods of monitoring and reporting risks

6.1.1 'Traffic lights monitoring'

This is a technique for evaluating the overall risk to a project schedule by a continuous assessment of the risk of its elements and their subelements. We have used it extensively and find it easy and convenient. It is basically a divide-and-rule technique:

1 List the key elements for assessment during the project.
2 Break key elements into constituent elements.

(You may want to use the risk factors table approach for these first two steps.)

3 Assess each second-level element on a scale.
   (a) On plan—colour green (G).
   (b) Not on plan but recoverable—colour amber (A).
   (c) Not on plan—recoverable only with difficulty—colour red (R).
4 Review all second levels to arrive at first-level assessment.
5 Use first and second levels to arrive at overall assessment of schedule and quality.

An example is given in Fig. 6.1. Colours would add emphasis to the chart.

6.1.2 Monitoring schedule by timeline

The project *timeline* (Fig. 6.2) is a powerful tool for monitoring project trends: it is also useful for the project plan and for monthly reporting. Too often, project activities slip one week, then another, and the overall impact is lost if you merely look at the status on the day, or the change since last time. The main selling point of the timeline is its ability to show you the trend throughout the whole project lifetime at a glance. Remember that real time runs down the chart, and planned time across it. This one will show you how all the major checkpoint plans are being

Ref.		Activity	Project name Status by week											Comments
			1 7	1 8	1 9	2 0	2 1	2 2	2 3	2 4	2 5	2 6	2 7	2 8	
001		Functional verification	G	G	A	A	A	R	R	A	A	A	G		
	a	Code arrival into FV	A	A	A	A	R	R	R	A	A	G	G		
	b	Quality of code	G	G	A	A	A	A	R	R	A	A	G		
	c	Progress of testing	G	G	G	G	A	A	A	A	A	A	A		
002		System test													
	a	Code arrival into ST													
		⋮													

Figure 6.1.   Monitoring on a weekly basis.

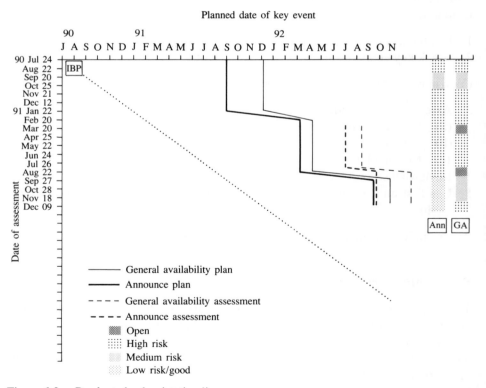

Figure 6.2.   Product checkpoint timeline.

kept. Down the right-hand side are traffic lights showing the risk assessed against each of the major checkpoints. It can be presented monthly with the monthly risk assessment.

6.1.3 Presenting risk reports at status meetings

This technique shows a neat way of presenting risk status in a concise way for a regular project status meeting, or even recording it in the product's working plan. This should contain at any one time a complete list of all the risks identified. For each risk should be detailed:

- Risk area
- Precise statement of risk
- Rationale behind the risk
- Priority in terms of management action required
- Management plan to remove the risk
- How long this item has been a risk
- How the plan is to control the risk tracking

In practice, there will be a threshold below which a risk is too insignificant to report.

A format that we have found useful for reporting risk in the project plan is the top 10 risk chart (Table 6.1), as described in Barry Boehm's paper (Boehm, 1988). As Boehm says, 10 risks are the most you can sensibly present at any one time, otherwise your audience will not see the wood for the trees.

A number between 7 and 12 is reasonable, but do not present everything on a regular basis. None the less, keep *all* the risks up your sleeve so that you can keep monitoring them, even if you only report the most significant on a regular basis.

A problem with this particular implementation is keeping tabs on how long something has been a high risk, or a risk at all. The importance of doing this is not that long-standing risks are necessarily the most important, but that many risks do become more important if left to fester, and it will be worth remembering how long risks have been around, and how long people have been promising to sort them out for you.

6.1.4 Monthly risk reporting for senior management

The more senior the management, the simpler must be the chart. The monthly report (Fig. 6.3) will summarize the top 10 chart by extracting the most important risks. It will be worth keeping a copy of that in the project plan too, so that the whole team can see what the project is telling senior management.

Table 6.1. Projex—HPA high risk list

Pos	Item at risk	Management plan	Who	Plan date	Deadline	OK
1	Jun availability schedule and quality is exposed because PRINT claims in general information manual are not being validated by current plan.	Re-announce function which is supported *and* ensure system test validation plan reflects new announce.	AJD	12 Dec 91	12 Dec 91	Y
2	No committed ProjX 2.2 or ProjY 1.3 delivery vehicle to contain ProjZ LU6.2 install changes.	Escalate lack of committed plan from other site to provide delivery vehicle	HSC	31 Oct 91	25 Dec 91	N
3	Quality certification may not be achieved for ProjZ.	Analyse current available data to estimate quality.	JKB	05 Nov 91	05 Nov 91	Y
4	Code quality may be unsatisfactory and cause service not to support shipment of ProjZ.	Prove final ship review requirements have been fulfilled.	NWL	31 Dec 91	31 Jan 92	Y
5	Product may not be ready to ship for Jun 90 availability. Must follow BS5750 requirements.	Produce BS5750 test completion reports for FV, ST, performance, usability.	NAA	25 Dec 91	25 Dec 91	N

Note: This table is intended to house *all* risks to successful project stage/component completion.

- *Pos*—position in table (indicates today's management priority).
- *Management plan*—plan agreed by management, following representation from risk assessment or other source, to control the risk.
- *Who*—which manager is responsible for controlling this risk.
- *Plan date*—date by which resolution is planned to be completed by the person named.
- *Deadline*—date by which resolution is required to avoid irreversible damage to schedule or quality (what the customer wants) as committed to lab management.
- *OK*—Is the management plan to control the risk running on schedule? The basis for this can be found in the status information of the person named in the 'who' column.

There is also scope for a medium risk table and a low risk list.

The plan dates are shown in Fig. 6.3(a), together with an assessment of whether the date is at risk or not, using the following terms:

- Open—the worst case, things are so bad that it is not even possible to calculate how bad they are: there is no viable plan.
- High—highly likely that you will not meet a major commitment.
- Medium.
- Low—unlikely that you will fail to meet the commitment.
- Good—no foreseen problems: almost certain to meet commitment.
- N/A—risk area does not apply to your product or has not been assessed.

Beneath the plan dates is an assessment of when the risk assessor believes the date will be if things go on the way they are. Beneath that is an indication of any plan reset which the project manager is planning, if any. If this box is filled in, the risk should be assessed against this new date, not the existing one. The second part of the table, Fig. 6.3(b), looks at the individual risk position

| Product assessment | | | | | | Assessed: 21 Nov 91 | |
| Product name | | | | | | Owner: A N Other | |

(a)

Checkpoint	#1	#2	#3	#4	#5	#6	#7
Risk			High			High	High
Plan	7/91	TBD	10/92	TBD	TBD	3/93	9/93
Assessed			6/93			9/93	3/94
Proposed							

(b)

Topic/risk	N/A	Good	Low	Medium	High	Open
Function			L	X		
Quality					X	
Process					X	
Business					X	
Resource				L	X	
Vendors	X					
Dependencies					X	
Constraints			X			

Basis for assessment

Function	Requirements for GLU-E not defined
Quality	Quality plan approval outstanding
Process	LA process is undefined
Business	Required support not available in DVA 5.7
Resource	Current planning based on staffing to headcount
	Skill shortage anticipated in 1Q92
Dependencies	DVA delivery vehicle agreements

(c)   Action plans

Due date	Who	Action
Dec 91	MGR	Recruit to positions
30 Jan 92	PMT	Define local availability (selected customers) process
		Status: Proposal submitted for review
*19 Dec 91	PP	Investigate inadequate business case impact on commitment checkpoint process
		Status: Date changed because of need to analyse options
19 Nov 91	PO	Investigate quality requirements
		Status: complete

Footer	Security classification	Initials

Figure 6.3.   Monthly risk report for senior management.

attached to each of the product 'abilities':

- Function—ability to deliver all the specified function
- Quality—ability to deliver quality commitments
- Process—exposures to the development process being used
- Business—exposure to the current business case

- Resource—exposures to the current and anticipated resource requirements
- Vendors—vendor's capability of fulfilling contractual commitments
- Dependencies—things you need from another organization to meet your commitments
- Constraints—external influences which you have no power to resolve

Indicate with an X what the current assessment is and with a letter matching the column heading what the previous month's assessment was, so that changes can clearly be seen.

Figure 6.3(c) lists the actions which are planned to try and influence, or control, the risks (not those lower than medium) with a date by which each action is to be taken (if this date is missed, additional impact can be expected), and the initials of the person who has accepted responsibility for taking it (this must be agreed before the chart is presented). If the due date is beyond the date of the next assessment, indicate how the item is progressing, and if it has changed since the last assessment, mark it '*', and say why the date has moved. On the report where the action is complete, leave the action on, and set the date to 'complete'. If there are no risks higher than 'low', leave the section on the report, but write 'none'.

As you assess each risk topic, you will build a set of backup information which will support your assessment. You should keep this safe, as you may be asked to justify your assessment.

6.1.5   *Risk assessment at checkpoints*

At checkpoints (as defined earlier) you may want something more substantial that looks specifically as far as the next checkpoint. We have used the model shown in Fig. 6.4. It is interesting how sudden pressures which seem unreasonable at the time can sometimes cause you to break new ground with unexpected benefits. Figure 6.4(a) is the background to the risk assessment, and Fig. 6.4(b) is the conclusion.

6.1.6   *Risks in tracking risks*

We have tried to point out the risks involved in adopting the procedures described in this book. There are risks in risk reporting, most of which have been pointed out in earlier chapters, but we summarize them here for reference (again, these points are addressed directly to the risk assessor, who may or may not be the project manager):

1   Getting hold of the right data from tracking systems, with accurate interpretation to base the assessment on.

2   Openness and honesty—getting accurate information from people. If you are going to report a risk and attribute blame to someone, it is right and proper to say so before the event, and to discuss with the individual a way of changing/

controlling/modifying the plan. Then you can present risk status with a united front. Avoid presenting risks at a meeting without first telling those involved; equally find out if the risk is likely to be resolved before you present it at the meeting.

3 Escalation—before you give an assessment, think ahead. What will happen if it is rejected? How far up the management line will you take it before you admit defeat, and which managers in the line will be interested to hear your assessment?

4 Parochial thinking—if you are doing the risk assessment for a product manager, make sure you know what is going to be important to them. Avoid large shopping-list risk reports, full of finicky problems. Focus instead on the big ones.

5 Reporting facts rather than opinion—all risk reporting is speculation about the future. Avoid opinions. Instead, produce sound logical arguments and information to back up each issue, based on relevant project or personnel history.

(a) Product Announce risk elements

A. Complete or not
B. Weeks behind plan today
C. Likelihood of completing late
D. Impact of lateness on GA
E. Dependency

		A	B	C	D	E	Notes
1.	High-level design	No			L		
2.	Code	No	3 + 2	M	M	10	
3.	FV	No	5	M	M	10	
4.	System test	No	0	M	H	10	
5.	PID validation	No	0	M	H	10	
6.	Usability	No	0	L	M	10	
7.	Performance	No	?	M	H	10	
8.	DOC'N production	No	0	0	0	0	
9.	DOC'N measurement	No	0	L	L	0	
10.	XXX driver	No	1	H	H	0	At least 7 weeks
11.	Quality prognosis	No				4	Cannot do today
12.	Quality exhibits	No	0	H		4	Refer to executive mgmnt
13.	Installation walkthru	Yes	0	0	0	0	
14.	Deliverables	No				5	
15.	DCRs	No	0				
16.	PTMs	No					
17.	PCFs	No					
18.	APAR migration	No					No trends visible
19.	Announcement	No	0	L	H		Needs expedition
20.	Serviceability	No	0	L	L		
21.	Service transfer	No	0	M	L		
22.	NLS	No					

Figure 6.4. Product announce risk elements and assessments. (*Continues.*)

(b)   Product   Risk element assessment

0   Highest risk item is lack of XXX driver, essential to a worthwhile announcement.
      —Many other items depend on this driver.
      —Previous document of understanding agreement was broken.
      —New strategic agreement at higher management level.
      —No detailed committed dates yet.
      Optimistic guess is that bug-free driver might be available by end November—7 weeks late.

0   Code is three weeks behind. Review trip to other site adds another 2 weeks to the critical path.
      Experience to date suggests addition of further week. Critical path therefore 6 weeks behind. This
      is an in parallel with the delay in the XXX driver.

0   No other perceived peculiar problems so add standard buffer of one week per month to end
      schedule. This is 6 months off, so add 6 more weeks. (Ref standard old-world philosophy.)

Grand total of 13 weeks, suggests general availability date of 2090 would be acceptable—provided firm
commitment from other site to get us complete bug-free driver by end November.

Pass lack of quality exhibits/prognosis to senior management for decision.

Shipment checkpoint should be held prior to shipment of product tape to ISD to ensure that all normal
announce checkpoint items are complete.

                                                                                          Date

---

Figure 6.4.   Product announce risk elements and assessments. (*Concluded.*)

6.2   Monitoring and reporting correctness

> Did you remember to cancel the milk and the papers, dear?

As with much of the material in these chapters, general risk management
techniques which are frequently practised by individuals in everyday life are either
totally forgotten in the workplace, or given quite pompous names when they turn
up in software development. But essentially they are the same. Verification and
validation are both based on the principle of two heads being better than one.
However much you think you know what you are supposed to be doing, and that
you are doing it right, someone else will always be able to spot something wrong,
or suggest an improvement. Even the simple act of reading your work to a
colleague can make you aware of an error that you would never have found on
your own.

Verification means simply comparing the output from a particular process stage
with the input to that stage, to ensure that you have translated it correctly and
completely. In ISO 9000-3 terms: 'Verification is the process of evaluating the
products of a given phase to ensure correctness and consistency with respect to the
products and standards provided as input to the phase.'

The question which introduced this section could be regarded as unfair if asked
by the husband of his new bride in the honeymoon suite, before any process or
ground rules have been agreed, but in the household where the 'going-on-holiday'

process is well practised and there is an agreed list of who does what, it is a valid piece of verification. The objective of the verification is to remove any defects at the time when they are least expensive to cure. Finding that the papers have not been cancelled when 30 000 ft over the Atlantic on the way to Barbados will be more expensive to cure than checking before leaving home. Waiting till the second week of the holiday to raise the question could be even more costly—you may have been burgled by then—and will totally demoralize your partner.

So, for verification to make sense, you need to have an agreed process with a start point and a deliverable. An example might be that you begin with a component design, and produce some code from it. The code can then be verified to ensure that it is an accurate implementation of the design. Verification should take place as soon as the deliverable is ready, and before proceeding to the next stage. The further you get into the next stage, the more it will cost you to resolve any defects you discover.

There are various kinds of verification in common use:

- Formal inspections
- Formal review meetings
- Less formal review
- Walkthroughs
- Buddy checks

It is not the purpose of this book to describe them fully, as there are plenty of other references which do that.

In the late seventies, we were introducing inspections into our own workplace, following the successful work by Michael Fagan in the USA. Some useful checklists were developed of 'things to check during an inspection'. It does not take a genius to realize that both morale and the quality of the product improve significantly if the inspection checklists actually become part of the development process. The developers can then use them as they develop; the same checklists are used during the inspection; and the inspection becomes more of a formality than a witchhunt. A 'no surprises' environment is good for morale and for quality programming.

Validation is another simple term, meaning 'to compare the output from a particular process stage with the customer requirements to ensure that the two match'. In ISO 9000-3 terms, validation is, 'the process of evaluating software to ensure compliance with specified requirements'. There is a subtle difference between these two definitions, because the second one contains the word 'specified'. The first definition suggests you keep checking on your way through the development that what you are doing matches what the customer wants. The second suggests that you ensure that what you are doing matches your written statement of what the customer wants. Looking back to the early eighties, the buzz-phrase was 'conformance to specification'. Compared with what had gone before, it was fine to try and achieve this, but, of course, there are several stages between the customer and the specification, and in each there is scope for deviation. The specification may not be a statement of what the customer wants, but the developers' view of what they want, adorned with flashy bells and whistles (and possibly omitting the wheels). With good validation and verification (V and V), the specification would resemble the requirements more closely, but now that customers are becoming more computer literate, it has become more sensible to liaise with them throughout the development to ensure that what is being developed is not deviating from what they want. You may also find that as you develop your product, what they want changes as the world moves on.

Validation is the mechanism for checking this. Ideally, it is performed by the customer, but it can be performed by planners or testers who have an intimate knowledge of the customer's requirements. It can take the form of a paper review, though a prototype is better, as the customer can try it for real. As with verification, the objective is to trap defects (deviations from the customer requirements) at the earliest opportunity, when fixing them is cheapest.

The main problem with V and V has been to persuade the designers and coders that it is worth doing. To them it is just extra effort. Their work is always 100 per cent right, so why bother to have it checked? Holding inspections just wastes their valuable time. The testers can find any problems later—it will not cost the designer or the coder any more.

It is therefore essential that the developers understand the economics of V and V, and why it makes sense to do it. It is essential that everyone is trained in inspection and review procedures, and good if you can have a pool of trained moderators. Calling an inspection needs to be easy; prebooked conference rooms are a help; and the procedure for recording the problems found needs to be slick to operate. An inspection recording tool we tried some years back took four hours to record the output from a two-hour inspection: that sort of procedure just gets the entire inspection process a bad name. An idea which is gaining currency, now that the cost of computing is dropping dramatically, is the 'knowledge mining centre'—a room fitted with workstations or terminals, where work can be inspected online and even changed as you review it.

All development stages are capable of verification and those where verification is omitted may be regarded as having introduced a risk. Many are also capable of validation.

One last thought on V and V: we believe (but cannot yet prove) that the way to reduce risk and ensure a high-quality product is for the software developers to take ownership of the work for which they are responsible, with objectives that clearly state that they are there to produce, not lines of code, but *correct* lines of code. Here, correct lines of code means lines of code with less than a given number of defects. Exactly how many errors are allowed is determined by the defect removal model (see Chapter 3). Once that number has been reached, any remaining errors (including those discovered by the customers) should be fixed in the developers' own time. Whether or not they choose to have verification and/or validation performed on their work should be entirely their choice, and they should be able to choose reviewers whom they consider to be the best to perform the job.

6.2.1   Risks in verification and validation

Forgetting the objective

As with all things, it is important to keep the objective in mind. Once the V and V process becomes so cumbersome that it is more costly to run than the saving in detected errors, some rethinking may be needed. One product with which we have been connected included in its test process a random test case generator, which could hammer code with all manner of permutations and combinations of input, and detect error after error. We were able to demonstrate for that project that it was cheaper not to inspect code, but pass it straight to the generator. Whether it would have been worth building the generator had it not existed already from previous releases is a different question.

Recent experience with inspections has suggested that rather than pick random inspectors, it maybe more profitable to employ full-time expert inspectors within the development team—very experienced developers who can carry a broad knowledge of the product in their heads, do not need to prepare for inspections, can be scheduled at very short notice, and reduce the inspection cycle time by a factor of 10.

Inadequate preparation

For inspections and reviews to run well, everybody needs to have been sent the material well in advance, and to have spent time looking at it and preparing comments. The chairperson or moderator should check this at the start of the meeting. However, there will be several experienced professionals who know so much that they can come to the meetings without preparation and contribute more fully than some who have. This is excellent. They could well be candidates for the post of full-time inspector described earlier.

The problems come from those who have less skill, but try to emulate their more senior colleagues by turning up at the meeting without preparation. They can quickly hold an inspection to ransom, by asking all sorts of questions of understanding which they should have asked the author privately beforehand. The moderator must be firm, and terminate the meeting once this starts happening. The immediate result will be a small slip in the schedule, but the embarrassment caused will ensure that it never happens again.

Straying from the objective

Some other common problems, broadly to do with straying from the objective of the meeting, can be avoided by ensuring that all review chairpersons are well trained. These include:

- Generally forgetting what you are supposed to be doing. Is this a verification? Of what against what?
- Straying outside the scope into things which were closed in earlier stages— rewriting the objectives during a code inspection for example.
- Fixing the problems. Early inspection theory said that it was bad to try and fix problems during the inspection, though there is now a school of thought which says that if there is a workstation or terminal in the inspection (knowledge mining centre), it is profitable to make small changes, where these can be done accurately within a few minutes.

The wrong people

It is important for the efficiency and effectiveness of the V and V process to ensure that it is performed by the right people. For validation, this is ideally the customer. For verification, useful candidates may be the owners of the previous and next stages, as they know the inputs and outputs. For large document reviews, a common failing is in getting a vast team of people to wade through the entire document. It is best if the author directs them to look at predetermined sections suited to their particular skill, and takes responsibility.

V and V takes time

Do not fall into the trap of assuming that coding takes the same time with and without V and V. When planning, allow person-hours for the author of work to have it reviewed, and for the reviewers to take part in the reviews. Also allow elapsed time for the reviews to be arranged, and the problems to be fixed.

7
Requirements

You might be tempted to think, during the requirements stage, that there are no risks till later in the project, when the test is half-way through and there are more defects than you expected and the end date is moving out one month every week. In fact, some of the most significant risks occur in the requirements stage, and it is worth thinking about why that is.

The requirements (and to a lesser extent, objectives) stage is different from the better known activities of software development, like coding. As we discuss in Part Three, risk management in this stage is more qualitative: the risks are (almost entirely) that the requirements gathered do not match the users' real needs, or are not sufficiently understood or articulated. This means that the risk manager has to be satisfied that the requirements that are defined represent a reasonable base from which to launch the rest of the project. Because of the qualitative nature of this work, it is not easy to be fully confident about this.

The answer, of course, is process. By defining the appropriate methods for gathering information, identifying classes of user to interview, and so on—and by putting appropriate controls on these activities, so that the deliverables are defined beforehand, and validated—then confidence is built up by virtue of the right things being done at the right time with the right people, in a predictable way.

The work that you do on reducing risk will, among other things, result in you finding defects in your requirements. Welcome these discoveries: defects uncovered at this stage, while probably few in number, are actually more valuable than those found later. Yes, it is useful to test the product, and discover that the columns in the monthly stock report are misaligned, and take the time and trouble to line them up again, but what if the customer did not want a monthly stock report, but a weekly graph? You have spent many person-months designing, coding and testing the function, and it may be wasted because it is not what the customer wanted. Not only will the expenditure have been wasted, but also there will be no return on your investment.

In Table 7.1 we have used the risk-factor approach, introduced in the early part of the book, to derive typical requirements risks. These risk factors can be

Table 7.1.   Risk factors in requirements

Primary questions	Secondary factors	Tertiary factors	Risk factors
Will the schedule be met?	Estimates wrong	Estimator's experience	Not enough time to do good requirements job
	Dependencies	Access to users	Information not available when needed
Will quality be acceptable?	Requirements	Definition	Not well understood
		Completeness	Omissions and/or redundancies
	Methods	Gathering, documenting	Inadequate methods and tools
		Validation	Defects not removed
	Quality management	Validation	No user involvement
		Personnel	Lack of skills and experience
Will function delivered be what is required?	Requirements definition	Prioritization	Inappropriate allocation of resources
		Currency	Solution not future-proof
	Project scope	Problem definition	Wrong problem being solved
		Strategy	Wrong solution being developed
		Change management	Inadequate control of change

associated with specific measures to control each, as in Table 7.2. Where a short explanation can be given it is shown in the table; otherwise, a reference is given to a later section in this chapter.

Thus the main classes of requirements risk are:

- The wrong people involved, at the wrong time
- Inadequate requirements gathering method
- Poor consolidation and validation
- Changes in requirements

Each of these is discussed in more detail below, together with a short case study.

7.1   Who and when in the requirements stage

7.1.1   *The marketplace, the customer and the user*

Do Rolls-Royce especially mind that you will not be choosing one of their cars when you replace your current one? Probably not, because you are not in the market segment they are trying to sell to. They understand their market, and pitch their products accordingly. It is important to begin requirements gathering by partitioning that segment of the world's businesses to which you would like to sell your product, so that you know from whom to gather requirements. Even for the

Table 7.2. Measures to take for development risk factors

Risk factors	Control method
Not enough time to do good requirements job	This is a difficult one. Historically, requirements have occupied a small proportion (say 5%) of the project duration. Some of the most successful projects have allowed the requirements to expand to as much as 40%, the rationale being that if the customer is engaged in specifying *exactly* what is required, and knows that is what will be delivered the actual development work goes very much more easily. We recommend that the requirements stage is allowed to float until it is apparent that there is convergence upon an agreed set.
Information not available when needed	Nominate a user representative, whose responsibility it is to ensure good liaison between development and user communities.
Not well understood	The developers need some means of demonstrating to the users that their ideas have been received and understood. Sometimes this can be done at this stage by prototyping; whatever method is used, the key is effective two-way communication.
Omissions and/or redundancies	Again, communication is the answer. The role of the user representative (see above) becomes vitally important here. See Sec. 7.3.3 for more information on requirements that can be overlooked.
Inadequate methods and tools	Although imagination and the ability to listen carefully are probably the most important tools that can be brought to the requirements stage (see Sec. 7.2 for information on requirements gathering methods), a requirements database that can be used for collecting, storing, prioritizing and tracking requirements reduces the workload and makes the task of administering the requirements much easier.
Defects not removed	Hold a verification/validation review, with the objective of getting a formal commitment from the user rep. that the requirements, as written, form the basis for the development (see Sec. 7.3).
Insufficient user involvement	The risk here is probably missed users, rather than no users. See Sec. 7.1 for more information on your user constituency
Lack of skills and experience	As indicated above, the main skills to bring are imagination and a good listening ear—not esoteric skills, but they do need to be cultivated carefully. Allow time. Experience is vital from the user side, and the user rep. should ensure that access is provided to the right people.
Inappropriate allocation of resources	This means putting effort into the wrong things. If you do not understand which requirements have most significance for your users, the solution you develop could be skewed away from the 'musts' to the 'nice-to-haves'. See Sec. 7.3 for more information on prioritizing requirements.
Solution not future-proof	As we said above, you need imagination—both you and the users. Try to create environments where ideas flow freely. Some of the practicalities of this are discussed in Sec. 7.1.
Wrong problem being solved	This is not really within the scope of this book, as it is more of a business concern, but it is something that the project team should be aware of— you might be fixing the tiles on the roof, when really the foundations need shoring up.
Wrong solution being developed	This one is very much an IT concern. Does the solution that is being requested, and its hardware/software implications, fit in with the strategic plans of the IT department?
Inadequate control of change	Change of requirements is always a problem—even (maybe especially) during the requirements stage. Be aware that both real needs can change (due to business circumstances) and users' perceptions of needs can change. The formal change control mechanisms of later stages are not appropriate here, but be aware of the need for your documentation methods to keep up—the requirements database is especially useful here.

in-house product, you should understand the characteristics of your customers and who to ask to supply requirements.

There is a quite unjustified belief on the part of many developers that they know better than the customer what the customer's real needs are. It can certainly add spice to the working day to specify a few attractive little add-ons; but it does absolutely nothing for the product. Do not allow a software developer to add requirements (unless the product is specifically designed to help software developers)—their contribution comes later.

If you have an existing customer set, you can pick a representative sample of customers. The far more difficult case is when you are in totally uncharted territory, with no existing user-base. Whatever the circumstances, there is always a risk that you ask too few customers, so that you fail to identify all the requirements; and the rather rarer risk of asking too many customers, so that you get repetitions and poor value for money.

A related risk is asking the customer and failing to ask the user. If you think of a software package for producing monthly stock reports, several different kinds of people have requirements of it, and you will be more likely to succeed if you can satisfy all of them.

Do not ignore any of these groups—they will not all have the same requirements:

Management	In all probability, they will be interested in the reports the product produces, the kind of decisions it helps them to make, and the ease with which they can get the reports.
Users	Those who have to use the system, feed the data in, and so on. They are likely to be interested in ease of learning, ease of use, functions offered, response time, reliability, and so on.
DP department	Interested in aspects of machine loading, response time, throughput, installation, migration, and so on.
Finance	How much does it cost? How quickly do we get a return on our investment?

7.1.2   Requirements versus objectives versus specification

This chapter is about requirements: what the customer wants or needs. (We use the singular 'customer' even though there are many people who should be regarded as users, as we saw above). Requirements are expressed by the customer, and should be validated by the customer. They should therefore be regarded as the property of the customer, no one else. They should not be confused with objectives and specifications.

Objectives come next and are your property, as the provider of the solution. They define the 'abilities' of the product you will make, and should be expressed in measurable terms, so that it can be demonstrated that the terms have been met. It is unlikely that the objectives will match the requirements in scope exactly. It may be unprofitable for you to fulfil every requirement listed. You may decide to omit some, or to set a goal which will only partly satisfy a need. That is up to you. In the objectives, you define what your development team must achieve to keep you in business: your goals.

The third item, the specification, is the property of the developers and defines how they will achieve the goals. (Objectives and specification and the risks they involve will be discussed in Chapter 8.)

7.2 Requirements gathering

It bears repeating: capturing, analysing and organizing requirements are the essential first steps in the development of a high-quality product. So, a significant risk in the requirements stage is the failure to find out what the customers think they want. Whatever we make must fit with the customers' own models of the world, their own way of working or doing business.

As we sit in our offices, using workstations and word processing software, we can theorize on what your office is like and how you do business, and we could design a software system which would allow you to write books too. But in all probability you would not like it. Perhaps you do not have a host-connected PC on your desk, perhaps your secretary does all your typing for you, perhaps you work from home, perhaps you have no desire to write books: other things we do not, and probably cannot imagine. So it is a risk not to try and meet some typical potential customers and walk in their shoes for a while to understand *their* model of the world, and how your product will fit into it.

The laid-back chat with the customer in the pub may seem the civilized way of finding out what you need to know, but the informal approach will not ensure the coverage that you need. By imposing some structure on the dialogue with the customer, the risk of an error in capturing requirements can be reduced. There are five key questions to be asked.

1   What do you want?

The aim is to get the customers to think entirely in their own terms, with their model of the world, and for you to listen to what is being said—not to barge in with your own preconceived list of product features. A few 'what-if' questions, based on your own understanding of what the technology can supply, may be appropriate, but at this stage *do not* translate what is being said by the customer into your own words. Leave it exactly as the customer said it.

If you think you are being told the solution rather than the requirement, try and steer the customer back to the requirement. For example, 'two-litre engine' is (probably) a solution; 'has good acceleration' is (probably) a requirement. The latter may be capable of fulfilment by the former or by various other solutions.

2   *Why do you want it?*

Once the customers have said what they want, the next classic error is to imagine that you know why they want it. If they want a two-litre engine, you may imagine that this has something to do with acceleration and speed, whereas in fact it could be because the company expense claim procedure says that owners of cars with engines of two litres or more can claim a significantly higher mileage rate than with 1999 cc engines, so two litres is what they want, and nothing less will do. However, once you know why they want it, and that it is a financial requirement, you can probably work out how to solve it some other way.

3   *How will you know when you have it?*

Again, asking this question can lead to unexpected insights into what lies behind the requirement statement, as well as providing a means of measuring the delivered function. You will often find that the answer you receive bears little relationship to the answers to the first two questions. Try it and see.

4   *How important is it to you?*

It is important to understand whether this requirement is a nice-to-have, or whether it is absolutely essential if the customer is to buy the product at all. When you start developing, you do not want to direct all your effort into the wrong item.

A scale which is often used in categorizing requirements is the following:

E   Essential—must have it or will not buy the product.
I   Important—key factor in the customer's decision to buy.
U   Useful—good value-add which will put your product ahead of the field.
N   Nice to have—cosmetic.
X   Do not want it—when you ask one customer about a requirement sugges-
       ted by another.
O   Other/do not care—maybe when the customer thought longer, it became
       obvious it was not important enough to fit into one of the other categories.

The term 'customer wants and needs' will be used later. You could say that categories E and possibly I refer to needs, and U and N to wants. X and O are of more use later when requirements are grouped and combined into a prioritized set. Then it is important to realize the difference between 'I do not especially want this requirement' and 'I definitely do *not* want this requirement'. Using the car example, the statements:

- It is very important to me that the car has a high top speed.
- It is not very important to me that it has a high top speed.

- It is very important to me that the car does *not* have a high top speed (my kids would probably wreck it).

are all very different.

5   *What are your perceptions?*

This question is to prompt customers to talk more about what they have today, about what they see your competitors doing, how they see technology advancing in the sphere of this particular requirement.

You will find that the customer has a number of 'wants and needs', and that you can write each on a separate sheet of paper. Do not interpret. Do use the customer's words. Use the format of the five questions, with a separate sheet for each customer.

7.2.1   Abilities

When quality was defined in Sec. 3.2, the term 'whatever property' was used. Open-mindedness was stressed. However, there is a risk that the statement of quality is so broad that you simply walk round in a mist asking people what they want, and never break the idea down into something which is useful to your developers.

The abilities list was introduced in Sec. 3.2, where it was said that it could be used time and again throughout the development cycle. From the start, you need to understand what the customer wants in each of these abilities, but this needs to be reflected right through the development, in the objectives, the specification, design, coding, publications and testing. Once you have defined the requirements, track them carefully against the stage deliverables until the project is complete.

If you look at the abilities list again, then refer to the list of requirements for your next car, in Sec. 7.5, you will see that the requirements given there each fit loosely into one of the 'ability' categories, more or less in the same order, but not with a one-to-one correspondence.

7.2.2   Practicalities of collecting requirements

You could simply send out questionnaires to everybody asking the questions described, but actually this is not the most productive way of doing it. The best bet is to invite groups of customers into a workshop session and do the following.

- Have them focus on an ideal world in which there are boundless possibilities for satisfying requirements.
- Put in some questions of your own to prompt discussion.
- Generate lots of requirements through the dialogue described in Sec. 7.2.

- Add in some of your own to see how the customers react, for example 'has low cost'.
- Ask them to pick out their 10 most important requirements.
- Have them prioritize on a scale of 1 to 10 how important they are in the context of the ideal system.
- Ask them to do the same for competitive products.

How many workshop sessions to run is an open question; there need to be enough so that no significant new requirements are being discovered and not so many that the process is becoming inefficient.

7.2.3   Get the requirements right

Gathering the requirements is the foundation for the whole of the rest of the project, maybe several person-years' effort from a team. Get it wrong and you destroy the morale of the team and expend a lot of money for little return. Take as long as you need. Think and plan well before you set out. Perhaps run a pilot study in-house to check that the principles work well before setting out to meet the customers. Know who the customers are and what they want, so you will know what their risks are, and make it your objective to minimize the risk.

7.3   Consolidation and validation

7.3.1   Grouping requirements

The output from the process described so far is lots of pieces of paper (one of our recent projects had 950), each with a separate requirement on it, and some priority and importance information. These need organizing into some structured form so that you can understand them. We do not intend to describe fully how to do this here, but there are some useful general principles that you can apply, typified in the 'power sort'. In summary:

1 Like requirements are clumped together.
2 Clumps of like requirements are grouped . . .
3 . . . to as many levels as necessary.
4 Statements in the customer's words are selected to identify the groups.
5 A tree is built as shown in Fig. 7.1.

For a thousand requirements, you will probably need a team of four with a clear leader, and a couple of days in a room with lots of big tables, plenty of space to walk round them, and an inexhaustible supply of sticky labels to identify the piles of paper you produce.

The final tree will be very similar to the risk factors table, in that the low-level items will be integrated together right-to-left to determine whether a car does match your ideal. One advantageous spin-off from having broken the requirements down in this way is that it becomes possible to measure them. Be assured

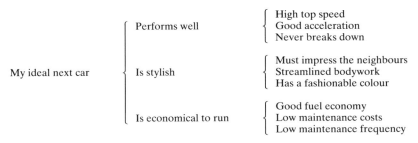

Figure 7.1.   Example of requirements grouping.

that even if you do not, your customers will. Their measurement is binary, satisfied, or not satisfied, and the overall result is also binary, buy or not buy. Defining measures is discussed in Chapter 3 and setting targets is discussed in Chapter 8.

7.3.2   *Prioritizing*

When you have a long list of requirements, how do you decide what the overall importance is?

1   You could simply add up all the weighting values they have individually given and divide by the number of customers.
2   You could ask all the customers to pick out their favourite 10 or 12 requirements from the grand total you have collected.
3   You could arrange what is known as a forced choice pairwise comparison. This is a heavy technique, best performed at a computer. You sit your customers down and ask each to compare every requirement with every other one, and decide which is more important to them. Each pair of requirements is flashed up on the screen in turn, randomly if possible, and they are asked to give an instant judgement of which is more important. The one which is more important has one point added to its running total in the system. The number of comparisons to be made is $n(n-1)$, so that is 90 comparisons for 10 requirements or 182 comparisons for 14 requirements, so bear this in mind when thinking how many requirements to present.

   The easy case is when you are only developing a product for one customer set (i.e. one user-representative), in which case the user representative's simple prioritization will suffice. If you have lots of customers, they will probably put different priorities on the requirements. Pick what seems the most appropriate method from the list above.

7.3.3   *Focusing on the wrong requirements*

The customer has already told you which requirements are believed to be the most important. Does this mean that you should devote the most effort to satisfying these requirements? Surprisingly, the answer is only a qualified yes.

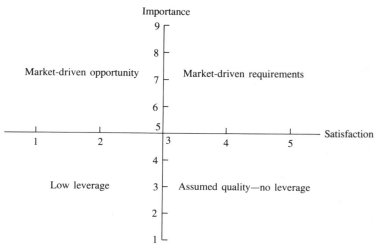

Figure 7.2.   Customer requirements matrix.

The reason is shown in Fig. 7.2, which is a sort of scatter chart. Each requirement is represented by a point on the chart. The position of the point is determined by the importance the customer places on the requirement and the current level of satisfaction with that requirement as fulfilled by other known systems. This may include the customer's current, possibly manual, system. The chart divides into four quadrants:

Top right   Here, the customer is highly satisfied with the current system, and it is very important to the customer. The competition does it well. You must do it well even to compete.

Top left   Here, the customer is not satisfied with the current system, but it is very important to the customer. The competition does not do it well. Focus on this kind of requirement, and your product will have a competitive edge.

Bottom left   The customer is not satisfied, but it is not important. For, example, I still have to read the manual when I program the video, but I still do it, and it would probably not influence my decision to buy significantly, because there are other thing about the video which are far more important. You can probably give these less focus.

Bottom right   Now here is the surprise—things which the customer has not rated as important, but with which there is satisfaction. An example of this is the clean glass in the restaurant. The 'industry norm' is to have a clean glass in a restaurant. You do not regard it as important: you are satisfied, but you will be indignant if you do not get it. Ignoring requirements in this quadrant is a significant risk.

A good knowledge of the competition and the marketplace is probably needed to recognize these. However, it is probably best not to consider them in great detail at this point, but to bring them in when dealing with objectives in the Chapter 8. At that point you can also include requirements from internal sources, like company IT strategy.

7.3.4 *Requirements verification and validation*

We introduced verification and validation in Chapter 6. They apply to all deliverables. The requirements statement is a deliverable, so verify it. That way you reduce the risk of having got it wrong. The verification in this case is simply to check that you have captured the requirement in the approved format, that the words written down are understandable by the kind of person who is next in the development process, and needs to be able to understand it, and to have a general sanity check that the requirements gathering appears to have been done in a disciplined fashion.

Validation can also be performed at this stage. You will recall that validation is about ensuring that the content of what you had written down still corresponds with what the customer wants. This should be relatively simple at this stage, but should also be checked before proceeding.

7.4 Requirements change

As you go through the rest of development, the world will change, the marketplace will change, and your customers' expectations will also change. That does not mean that you instantly react to every change that is suggested, redesign, churn the product round, and so extend the development schedule. Nor does it mean that you plough on regardless, sticking to your original requirements set. The recommended approach is in between and has three essential characteristics:

1 As you leave the requirements phase, you freeze the product content, that list of requirements which will be in the final product.
2 You keep the requirements channels open with a process which is as good as the one you used to collect the requirements in the first place.
3 You institute a change management process, so that you can critically evaluate which of the new requirements should be included in your product and which should be ignored. This must have all that your original selection process had, and a more stringent set of selection criteria, as you are now further down the line.

It is highly risky not to control this change process properly.

Keep referring back to the 'abilities' list and keep aware of the way the different abilities will change if a new requirement is added. Be especially aware of availability and cost, as too much change will extend your schedules and increase the cost of development and either the price or the profitability. Adding new function may delay the availability of the product with significant impact on the business case. You may do better to run a slick development process, get version one out quickly and follow up with version two containing all the new requirements. You will be able to start developing version two before you finish version one and gain a time advantage.

You may also need to refer back to the customer who generated the requirements if you are thinking of change. It is therefore essential that your individual requirements carry the name of the originating customer, and the name of the person who transcribed the requirement to paper.

A final word about requirements change: beware of your director of programming playing golf with senior customer executives and returning next day to direct you to incorporate a new requirement they have requested. Ensure that, like all other requirements, it goes through all the procedures described in this chapter. You can do this seriously and genuinely without being offensive, because you 'wish to make sure you get it right'.

7.5   Case study

This illustrates the techniques described, based on the purchase of a car. Different requirements are expanded using the five key questions.

1   Very reliable

- What do you want? I want a car which always gets me where I want to go.
- Why do you want it? A car is a means of getting me somewhere. If it fails to do that too often, I would be better to plan some other way of doing it.
- How will you know when you have it? Never fails to start, never fails on the road especially in a life-threatening way. All problems found during planned routine servicing.
- How important is it to you? Very important.
- What are your perceptions? Advertising is economical with the truth. I cannot guarantee to get high reliability even if it says I will. Wide variations—Friday afternoon cars, etc.

2   Needs little maintenance

- What do you want? I want a car which needs little maintenance.
- Why do you want it? Because I do not service my own car—every time it goes for servicing, I lose it for a day, and have to catch the bus to work.

- How will you know when you have it? Only two services each year.
- How important is it to you? Very important
- What are your perceptions? Some cars seem to have longer service intervals than others. Parts seem to be more expensive for some cars than others.

3 Will take family and holiday luggage

- What do you want? A car to fit four people and all their luggage.
- Why do you want it? So I can use the car to go on holiday.
- How will you know when you have it? People and luggage will all fit.
- How important is it to you? Useful (could be a good excuse to holiday on my own!).
- What are your perceptions? Some cars seem to have fitted roof racks, and others have a more convenient tailgate than mine does.

4 Comfortable to drive for long distances

- What do you want? A car which I can drive in comfort for long distances.
- Why do you want it? So I can make journeys of 300 miles without feeling exhausted.
- How will you know when you have it? When I arrive and do not feel mentally drained and with aches and pains all over my body.
- How important is it to you? Important.
- What are your perceptions? Having driven many cars on business, I know that some are far more comfortable than others. A short test drive will not tell you this. (The producer might think about trying to make the car a fleet car.)

5 Has good quality inexpensive music

- What do you want? A car I can play music in while I drive along.
- Why do you want it? Car travel is pretty boring, and it is an ideal opportunity to listen to music—helps keep you awake too.
- How will you know when you have it? I will be able to play my tapes and listen to radio with good reception.
- How important is it to you? Important.
- What are your perceptions? My car radio cannot receive FM signals—useless now the classical program is not on MW any more. They tell me you can have CD players in cars nowadays. Reception is bad on my current car as the aerial keeps being vandalized and I have given up and started using a wire coathanger instead.

Now, the purists would probably say that cars and programming are (pardon the pun) streets apart. But this is by no means true. Using stock control as a programming parallel, the list given above would be something like:

- Very reliable
- Needs little maintenance
- Will handle all the product lines I have, and all the details I wish to record about them
- Easy to use for long periods at a time
- Has good quality online help.

As an exercise, you might like to answer the five questions for each of these attributes from the customer viewpoint.

8
Objectives and specifications

You may think that devoting separate chapters to requirements and objectives/ specifications is overemphasis: a disproportionate amount of material early on, when far more significant risks lurk waiting in the more visible later stages of the project. In fact the usual perception of project activity—a quiet beginning, followed by more and more frantic activity—is exactly the reverse of the model as it should be. The life cycle of a software development project should be like that of a river: tumbling, turbulent and dynamic (but small in volume) in the rarefied heights early on; gradually becoming more ordered, predictable, and increasing in size, until it flows broadly and placidly (though still marked by the occasional eddy at changes in direction) towards the sea of users.

The purpose of this chapter is to help control the fledgling project, to mark the change from mountain torrent to stream running through alpine meadows. We said earlier that the requirements are owned by the users, and the objectives are owned by you: this, in itself, is a good enough reason for the separate chapter, as meeting the objectives is what you will be judged on, and it is in your interests to be in control of your commitments.

We begin with a modern parable.

Now we know what our car-buying customers want, let us give it to them. Where is that requirements database? Let us see. There is a fairly even spread of engine sizes wanted. About 10 per cent want a 900 cc engine; the most popular size seems to be around 1600 cc; and a handful of people want a 3 litre job. So it is obvious that we must prepare a product with 10 different versions, one for each engine size. Oh, and there is also a requirement for a pedal version from the green lobby, who would like to be able to switch the engine off going down hill, and pedal until they cannot maintain the speed, so pedals had better be a separately orderable feature.

Now we come to the wheels: most people want four, but some want only three. Some want four-wheel drive, and I suppose for consistency we should offer a three-wheel drive capability on the three-wheeler too. So that makes 4 options to go with the 10 versions.

Then there is servicing. Most people want a reliable car, but about five per cent of the customers are DIY freaks, and would quite like a car which breaks down a lot, so they can escape from the household chores and hide under the bonnet for a while at the weekend. So we had better make sure that five per cent of the batch are less reliable than the rest, and we will need a dealer network to match these with the DIY freaks.

And so, after a while, we arrive at the universal product which is all things to all men (UP and ATTAM). It has so many versions that it is not possible for the dealers to stock one of each. You cannot order it yourself because you need a master's degree in bureaucracy to fill the form in. If you did manage to acquire one, it would come with the components in a separate package, so you would have to take several days (called 'installation time') to put it together before you could use it. You would then find that the manual telling you how to use it ran to 683 pages, and that every time you wanted to use the left/right indicator you had to stop the car and look at the manual to find out how to do it. And by the way, the word 'indicator' is not in the index.

No, the motor industry does not work like this, does it? But looking around, one often sees software being delivered in this way, for no particularly good reason, save that the developers tried to incorporate every requirement of every potential customer into the product, and thereby made something which was far too complicated for anyone to use without a long learning-curve.

The product objectives, the main subject of this chapter, are the statement of what you intend that your product will do, and the manner in which it will do it. They should be a translation of what the customers say they want (described in their terms), into a set of measurable objectives for the product in terms that programmers will understand. Basic costings are made to ensure that you know how much it will cost you to do it, and a business case is produced to show how much money you think you will make from it.

The product specifications are associated with the objectives in this chapter because the risks are similar: both are owned by development, both have a high proportion of qualitative work, and both are unique pieces of work, with none of the repeatability associated with the later stages of the project. The specifications provide the technical basis from which the design proceeds, and cover:

- The product as it will appear to the user
- The technical aspects of the solution

so there is a strong creative element in this stage. It is for this reason that specifications are combined with objectives here.

The standard risk factors table approach is used here to derive objectives and specification risks, in Table 8.1. These risk factors can be associated with specific measures to control each, as in Table 8.2. Where a short explanation can be given it is shown in the table; otherwise, a reference is given to a later section in this chapter.

The fundamental risk in all this is that you fail to achieve the basic objective, that is, to translate what the customer said into a good set of programming objectives for a product which will be profitable. In this stage, you need to:

- Investigate and understand the various ways of fulfilling the customer requirements, phrase these in objective terms for the programmers, and understand the implications of each of the alternative solutions offered.

Table 8.1. Risk factors in objectives/specifications

Primary questions	Secondary factors	Tertiary factors	Risk factors
Will the schedule be met?	Estimates wrong	Estimator's experience	Not enough time to do good objectives job
	Management pressure	'Progress' requested	Enter development too early
	Development team	Skills	Skills not available
Will quality be acceptable?	Objectives	Definition	Objectives not measurable
		Completeness	Omissions and/or redundancies
	Specification	Definition	Specifications do not model user interface
		Completeness	Omissions and/or redundancies
	Methods	Translating requirements to objectives	Inadequate methods and tools
		Validation	Defects not removed
	Quality management	Validation	Insufficient user involvement
		Control of objectives	Not being able to track objectives
Will function delivered be what is required?	Objectives definition	Selection and prioritization	Inappropriate product definition
		Mistranslation	Objectives (or specifications) do not match requirements
	Specification	Technical feasibility	Solution unrealizable
		Currency	Solution not future-proof
		Product appeal	Lack of imagination in product objectives
	Project scope	Sizing of solution	Delivery timing wrong for market/customers
		Strategy	Solution does not fit in with strategy
		Justification	Product does not have strong enough business case
		Change management	Inadequate control of change

- Decide exactly which requirements you will and will not fulfil. For example, if only one of your customers wants three wheels, is it really sensible to develop a separate version for just that one customer? It may be, but you need to evaluate it properly.

In Appendix 5 there is a template which we have used for presenting product objectives. It is fairly heavy because it was developed for an environment in which software was developed for customers worldwide with a large variety of operating environments. Many of these may not be variables for you, in which case you can prune the template down to suit your needs.

Table 8.2.   Measures to take for objectives risk factors. (*Continues.*)

Risk factors	Control method
Not enough time to do good objectives/ specifications job	This is a risk that was referred to in Chapter 7, but here the work is more predictable, in that you are working from an established base of requirements, with procedures and methods to effect the translations to subsequent levels of detail. The risk factor here is that not enough time is allowed for the creativity that is necessary for a really satisfactory solution. Look for your most successful (in the users' eyes) projects from the past, and see how much time was expended by them on these stages.
Enter development too early	The only way to control this risk is through process. Define the deliverables that you want from your objectives and specification stages, in enough detail that there can be no argument over the content, and then verify that the deliverables are correct. A complete process definition will have entry criteria for each stage: the criteria for starting development should include specifications complete and verified to the level of detail that you think appropriate.
Skills not available	This is an example of the 'limits-of-performance' risk. Support by providing training, from the many means of delivery available. The ideal training is 'just-in-time' and requires significant planning effort. Be wary of 'on-the-job' training that is often a euphemism for a money-saving exercise. 'On-job' learning can be little more than reading manuals and (supposedly) learning by making mistakes, with all the implications for wasted time, rework, frustration, etc. that implies. This is a pity, because the approach is a viable training option. Careful planning is needed, with a system of mentors responsible for individual trainees.
Objectives not measurable	This is one of the most challenging aspects of objectives-setting. For each objective, try to decide on the characteristic that is going to be most significant to the customers, and ask them how they will judge it. Devise a measure that will allow you to demonstrate that you have met the target. Often, a binary yes/no on a factor being present will meet the need. 'It is very difficult to measure' is no excuse. If you do not measure it, the customer certainly will, implicitly if not explicitly. For further guidance, see Chapter 3.
Objectives— omissions and/or redundancies	The 'abilities' list introduced in Sec. 3.2 can be used as a double check that you have not forgotten anything. Having listed all the requirements, you can try grouping them by ability. You may find that some of the ability groups are a bit sparse and can check if any have been missed. Another area to check is the satisfaction/importance matrix, introduced in Fig. 7.1. One quadrant represents 'assumed quality', things the customer will want, but not tell you about. It is worth taking time, perhaps aided by the abilities list and some market intelligence, to think of some things which the customer might not have asked for, but will expect. The compatibility, reliability and maintainability categories will be especially important, as the customer will expect your product to work with everything, and never fail.
Specifications do not model user interface	It is essential that the specifications model the way in which the user will interact with the system: the screens and reports, related to the different functions that will be available. See Appendix 5 for a template that models the contents of a specification document.
Specifications— omissions and/or redundancies	The best way to insure against this risk is to prototype the product: let the customer try the look-and-feel of the interface, while simulating the function. If this cannot be done, you could try developing user scenarios, with mockups of the screens involved, and walk the customers carefully through each scenario. Whatever method you use, you must involve the customer directly.

Table 8.2. Measures to take for objectives risk factors. (*Continues.*)

Risk factors	Control method
Inadequate methods and tools	There is a powerful tool that helps with the translation of requirements into objectives, see Sec. 8.2.
Defects not removed	As for requirements. Hold a validation review, with the objective of a formal commitment from the user representative that the objectives, as written, define a product that meets their requirements.
Insufficient user involvement	This is still the responsibility of the user representative, who was referred to in Chapter 7, who should be aware of the need for on-going effective liaison throughout the project.
Not being able to track objectives	The project tries to fulfil as many of the customers' requirements as practicable. You can avoid arguments about what individuals think the objectives *should* be if everyone can focus on what the customer has asked for. It is therefore important that: • The requirements are not thrown away at this stage, but are retained on a database to which the whole team has access throughout the project. • Every objective contains pointers to the requirement which spawned it. Indeed, this backward pointer practice can continue throughout all of the intermediate deliverables as the product is developed. That way, when there is debate concerning an objective, a specification, code, or test case, you can always return to the original requirement and obtain the real reason for what you are doing. Conversely, if a requirement changes later, you can always use a text-scanning program to discover all the elements which are there solely to satisfy that requirement, and make appropriate changes.
Inappropriate product definition	This risk results from wrongly subsetting the requirements that can be fulfilled from a long list. The right subset will not always be the top part of a prioritized list, as different line-items will have very different efforts associated with them, and these estimates may change depending on what other line-items are included. Arriving at the 'best' product objectives will therefore be an iterative process that heavily involves the user representative.
Objectives (or specifications) do not match requirements	This is exactly the sort of risk that the inspection process was defined for. In an inspection, a piece of work is carefully checked against the preceding level to ensure that the translation to the next level of detail has been done correctly. It is a comparison to detect errors of translation, omissions, and redundancies.
Solution unrealizable	It is a perennial blindspot of the IT industry that it tends to forget the KISS (keep-it-sweet'n'simple) principle, and embrace the latest technology and complex designs. Dependency upon delivery of the latest kit, or the realization of ultrasophisticated designs adds hugely to the risk.
Solution not future-proof	Using your privileged position in the IT industry, introduce (in a controlled manner) at this stage all those trends of which you are aware, and your customer may not be. Phrase them as possible objectives, and see how they count towards meeting the stated requirements. If they are good value for money, build them in.
Lack of imagination in product objectives	Imagining the answer without reading the requirement is wrong. Failing to use your imagination where it is really needed is equally wrong. Imagination is needed in dreaming up all the possible ways in which the requirement can be fulfilled. This is a time for exploration, invention, and discussion—several heads are better than one. Brainstorming techniques can be applied to generate ideas.

Table 8.2. Measures to take for objectives risk factors. (*Concluded.*)

Risk factors	Control method
Delivery timing wrong for market/ customers	It may be that a subset of the requirements can be achieved in a timeframe that will secure some advantage for you: in a competitive situation, early arrival on the market will secure a customer base; in a commercial situation, in-house, an evolutionary approach, rather than revolutionary (big bang) is often far more acceptable in a number of ways—cut-over is not so traumatic, some benefits can be realized earlier, and early experience allows for feedback into the architecture.
Solution does not fit in with strategy	A product is often only part of a total solution, and where this is so, you should consider how your product relates to an existing strategy. For example, response time for your program to process a transaction may be just a component in the response time as perceived by the customer, which could include the time for the transaction to be sent over a network, interrupt time, time for other programs in the loop to operate, and so on. What the customer requests as a response is the sum of all these. Your performance objective must take this into account, and the transaction time allowed your programmers may be just a small fraction of the response time requested by the customer.
Product does not have strong enough business case	To minimize this risk, hold the first checkpoint. You now know what you are going to make, how much it will cost and what profit you expect to make. So take this business proposal to your management, and convince them to fund you as far as the next checkpoint, the commitment checkpoint, by when you will have the product completely specified, and all your team planned and committed to finish the product by a particular date. At all costs, do *not* commit the end date yet as you do not know exactly what you are making: remember, no commitment, no risk.
Inadequate control of change	As we said in Chapter 7, change of requirements is always a problem. Now is the time to institute the formal change control mechanism. At a minimum, this should identify the request uniquely, describe it, and justify it. The developers should then cost the effort in making the change, and estimate the impact on the schedule and costs. If there are many change requests, they should also be prioritized. The user representative should then decide whether to accept the cost, or not. Sometimes, trade-offs may be possible in rebalancing the function delivered to take account of change and keep within the budget. See Sec. 8.3 for a method of monitoring change requests to see if the backlog is becoming unmanageable.

8.1 Quantitative objective-setting with QFD

Quality function deployment (QFD) is a technique for turning prioritized customer requirements into a set of meaningful product objectives which can then be deployed through all the organizational functions of your development team. The Japanese began to put effort into developing the technique about 25 years ago: in fact, Yoji Akao was funded by the Japanese government to develop the technique. Some years later, western industry caught on and started to use the technique too. The Ford Motor Company in the USA was a pioneer. IBM's use of the technique is more recent still. This section merely summarizes how to start using the process. A fuller description appears in the book by Bob King (1989), which you are recommended to consult if you want to use the technique in earnest.

Another useful reference is Hauser and Clausing (1988). Ford Motor Co. have also developed a tool called QFDPlus which will help you use QFD.

The central feature of the QFD technique is a chart known whimsically as the 'house of quality', simply because the chart looks a bit like a house. Information is stored in the 'left- and right-hand wall', the 'floor', and the 'ceiling'. The central and 'roof' voids are used as matrices for recording relationships between individual pieces of 'wall' and 'ceiling' information.

The objectives of the QFD process are to:

* Establish design targets for the product being developed.
* Improve communications between all development groups.
* Direct intellectual activity at the most important or critical areas.

8.1.1 Entry criteria

1 A set of market or customer requirements, like those generated in Chapter 7. Ideally these should consist of:

   (a) A want/need statement, e.g. 'performs well'.
   (b) Its importance to the customer/market in the range 1 to 9.
   (c) The perception from the customer of how the competitive or alternative product under analysis meets this want/need. It is a number in the range 0 to 5, with 5 being meets this requirement very well, and 0 being does not meet this requirement. The intermediate values are 1, very badly, 2, badly, 3 is the median, and 4 is well.

   If you are doing something innovative, the competitive process may just be the manual way your customers do it today. If you are being really innovative, like inventing the spreadsheet, you may have to do some soul searching to find the competitor, but it is still worth trying.

2 A QFD team. The team should be 6 ± 3 in size, and comprise individuals from different parts of the development process, such as market analysis (a person from the team which gathered the requirements—fairly essential), design, development, test, publications, human factors, tools, and build and integration. The roles of leader/facilitator and scribe should be assigned. The leader as a minimum should be QFD trained, and at least one member should have QFD experience.

   Steps

Refer to Fig. 8.1 for the parts of the house of quality that correspond to the numbered steps that follow:

1 Enter the requirements data (want/need, priority, and customer perception) into the left- and right-hand walls of the house, one to a row.

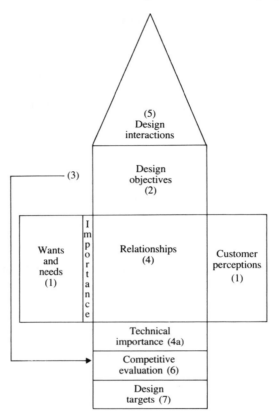

Figure 8.1.   A schematic QFD house of quality chart. The numbers refer to the order of steps used.

2   Generate the set of design objectives (also known as product characteristics or quality characteristics) on the 'first floor of the house'. These are design metrics which reflect the wants and needs. Typically these are such things as desk space, steps to perform, fields per screen, and time to perform. You make them by thinking about each requirement in turn and devising one or more quantifiable objectives which would fulfil the requirement. Sometimes it is difficult to generate a metric which is quantifiable and a binary (yes/no) metric has to be used. These should be avoided if possible, and can indicate a need for a subchart on this area. Reserve a column for each objective.

   For example, the 'want and need' asks for backup capabilities. At a first pass, one might set a yes/no metric (we do or do not provide backup) or use a 'steps to perform' metric. In fact, there are a number of metrics for backup/ restore that could be expanded on a subchart, leaving the yes/no metric on the main chart.

3   Ask competitive evaluation to evaluate the competitor products' performance in these design requirement metrics. These are fed back at step 6.

4   Generate the relationships. This entails examining each intersection of want and need and design objective to determine if there is a relationship between each want and need and each design objective. The relationships can be strong, medium, weak, or none, and are arrived at by asking: does design requirement X impact (either positively or negatively) 'want and need' Y? If no, leave blank. If yes, then is the impact weak, moderate, or strong?

When the the matrix has been completely traversed, some simple arithmetic will provide an evaluation of the technical importance of each design requirement.

5   Generate the design interactions. This is very similar to the previous step. Each design objective is compared to every other design objective, this time taking into account the direction of the interaction, i.e., whether the impact is negative or positive, but just using strong or weak.

6   Now is the time to get the feedback from competitive evaluation initiated in step 3 and enter the data into the chart. Next comes the analysis of all this data. The following serves as a checklist of items to watch out for:

Phenomena	*Possible actions*
Blank or 'weak' row	A customer requirement not being addressed; check for missing design objective(s); validate requirements.
Blank or 'weak' column	Superfluous design objective; remove it; validate requirements.
Anomaly between customer perceptions and competitive evaluation	Determine reason for anomaly; something does not compute; something is not understood properly.
Negative interactions between design objectives	Make sure these are communicated to the development teams; schedule brainstorming sessions to create breakthroughs to circumvent them.
Positive interactions between design objectives	Take into account when determining development plan. This may mean you can get something for nothing.

7   The final step of this stage is to set design targets for each of the design objectives. This is done taking into account the importance of the customer wants and needs; the customer's perception of how these are being satisfied; the technical importance of each design objective; and where the product is on the competitive evaluation relative to the competition. The basic criterion is 'where is the optimum place to spend the next allotment of development effort?'

You can also arrange all your design targets in groups, for instance by CUPRIMD (see Table 3.1) category, and get some more value out of the chart. If, for example, you find that you have no characteristics in the 'usability' group, this may indicate that you have missed something.

This is just the beginning of QFD activity, the highest level house of quality. As the development progresses, walls and floors of one house can be taken out and put into another house to allow other comparisons to be made. For example, the test team might want to map customer requirements against test cases, or design objectives against possible failure modes. The use of a QFD tool makes this transportation simple.

8.2   Coping with change

The perfect project—where the requirements are well defined early in the project, and then set in concrete—is an impossible dream. The sad fact is that we live in the real world, and that world changes around us. We have to keep up with it, and that means that plans have to change. The specification stage is where the product takes shape, and that shape is likely to be buffeted by the winds of change.

That is why design-change request (DCR) systems are needed; we recognize that change must happen, but we wish to keep it under control. We also make allowance for an expected level of change by budgeting for it in our plans. However, there is always the risk that excessive DCR activity will delay the end of code/unit test and functional verification. Our own experience is that high DCR activity will impact testing progress and entry to system test, and that change is nearly always underestimated.

The objective of this monitoring activity is to show the backlog of DCR work still waiting to be processed, i.e., is the DCR backlog large enough to impact development and test groups later?

8.2.1   Data

The number of DCRs in each state is plotted (see Fig. 8.2) on a weekly basis as a surface chart, with those in an active state where the actual work to be done by developers in changing the design and/or changing code (i.e., approved and committed) is below the x-axis whereas those which could cause extra work (i.e., new and proposed) are above the x-axis. Each surface gap shows the number in each state.

8.2.2   Interpretation

It is assumed that the volume and current status of DCRs are valid measures of the workload involved in changing the specification, design or code and that the change workload needs to be known so that development workload can be assessed. If the DCR rate shows a trend upwards or downwards then this can be used to predict the end of major DCR activity.

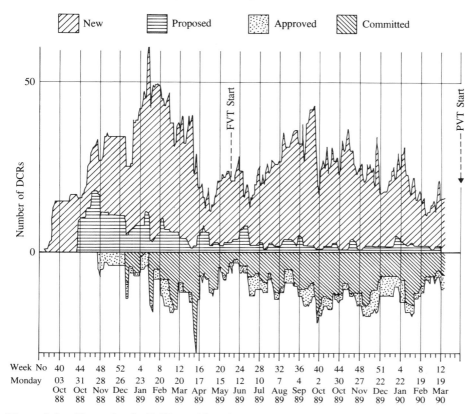

Figure 8.2.   Example of a DCR tracking chart.

Variations on this basic chart are:

1   The number of DCRs in each state are plotted as a surface chart where those in an active state (i.e., new, proposed, approved, and committed) are shown above the x-axis and those that are closed (i.e., deferred, rejected, and complete) are shown below the x-axis. Each surface gap shows the number in each state. This chart does have the advantage that it shows the rate of closure of DCRs (i.e., the development capability to complete work).

2   A better way of tracking the extra workload is to estimate the workload (in KLOCs, person-days, functional points, etc., of effort) when a DCR is submitted. Certainly the workload should be agreed by management (development and test) before the DCR is approved. This effort can then be tracked as a similar chart with the same categories, but each surface gap would be estimated workload in the DCRs instead of raw DCR numbers. Another useful chart would be one showing cumulative effort added to development workload per week because of DCR activity.

This is one of those frequent instances where correcting the problem is more difficult than recognizing that a problem exists. Where the change activity level is becoming unacceptable, then the users of the system (or, more probably, those that represent them) will have to be faced with some hard truths. Some horse-trading will have to be done between delivery of function and delivery schedule—but this just injects a little interest into a project manager's routine life.

Part Three
MORE—managing the optimum risk environment

In this part, we look at each of the major activities in the development of software. The division is somewhat arbitrary, and will not match everyone's process, but you will be quite familiar with each of the activities:

- Developing the product (Chapter 9)
- Testing the product (Chapter 10)
- Delivering the product (Chapter 11)

The type of risk management work during these stages is quite different from that done in creating the optimum risk environment (CORE). There, the work tended to be more qualitative or creative: the stress was on defining the product well enough to meet the foreseeable needs of the user, and tailoring (changing) the process to address the major risks, so that the likelihood and/or importance of the risks were minimized.

In this stage, the work is more quantitative. The process has already been adjusted to bypass the major risks. What is being done here is the collection of data to gain insight into the containment of the medium risks, and to monitor the minor risks. Essentially, risk management here is tracking.

The possible risks are myriad, and in a book like this we cannot possibly cover them all. What we can do is to cover the tracking methods to contain the types of risk that are most common in our experience. In practice, the approaches illustrated can usually be adapted to a variety of circumstances, so you should be able to regard them as models for your own purposes.

As we indicated in Chapters 7 and 8, the hard work of risk management in a successful project is done in the early stages. That is now behind you: you are on more familiar territory, and you have the confidence of knowing that your course is now mapped out for you by the RMP. Follow it, enjoy it, and learn from the experience. You will need to recall all that hard-won experience for the last part of the book, learning from the optimum risk environment (LORE).

9
Development

9.1   Working with the left side of the brain

Psychologists think of the brain as having two distinct halves, each with its own characteristic way of processing information. The right side of the brain works in a global, intuitive mode, seeing the big picture and coming up with imaginative, off-the-wall solutions. The left side works in a logical, analytical way, being happier with proceeding step by step. Of course, both of these characteristics (equally important in their own way) are present in everyone, but each will have his or her own particular blend, dictating a preferred way of working and thinking.

The development work covered in this chapter should be predominantly left-brain work. The really creative (right-brain) work is needed during the requirements/objectives/specification stages, when a lot of time is spent in finding out exactly what the customer wants, defining it, and working out how it can best be achieved. Now the work actually has to be done to realize the visions of the previous stages.

If the risks inherent in the creative stages have been avoided, then the risks inherent in the development work are characterized differently—as *process* risks. Which is not to say that the earlier work should not have been done through a process—of course it should. The volume of work will increase markedly during development, as development goes to lower and lower levels of detail and, to maintain project control, the original units of work need to be subdivided into more and more tasks. These tasks (similar in size and nature within each stage of development) will be more repeatable in a manufacturing sense. The planning, control and performance of these volume processes is more left-brain oriented, but with a good leavening of right-brain to come up with imaginative solutions to problems that crop up on the way.

It is worth exploring the concept of software a little more. With the vision of the product completely defined, its realization (development) should be as economical and predictable as possible. During the Industrial Revolution, economy and predictability were achieved by process and production lining, and these basic principles have been improved and refined ever since, first by the Western world and, more recently, by the Japanese in particular. Newer concepts such as standardized components and specialized tools have helped more.

The manufacturing of software has still a long way to go before it reaches the sophistication of, say, consumer goods manufacturing, but progress is visible. The software development process (in whatever form) is becoming more repeatable, and developments such as CASE are providing developers with the tools to do their job in a more controlled and effective manner. Software reuse, though still in its infancy, holds out the promise of standardized components that can be used off the shelf.

The concept of repeatability in manufacturing has to be stretched slightly to fit the software development scene, but there are the parallels referred to above:

- Tools
- A process
- Individual units of work of similar nature

There are ways of adjusting for the varying size of the units of work, in the statistical treatment of a manufacturing process, so the manufacturing analogy has value in this context.

Thus when we consider the risks in development, we should be considering process risks; the risks, in fact, of loss of repeatability. Process risks will typically be those associated with *volumes*: the risk of variation (of some attribute) among a large number; the risk of underestimating the productivity of the process in producing large volumes; the risk of undesirable trends in the production runs; the management of the people involved in the process, etc.

These ideas are developed into a risk factors table in Table 9.1. These risk

Table 9.1. Risk factors in development

Primary questions	Secondary factors	Tertiary factors	Risk factors
Will the schedule be met?	Estimates wrong	Estimator's experience	Systematically low estimates
	Code productivity low	Skills	Inherently low productivity
		Tools	Long learning-curve Inappropriate tools
	Plans wrong or incomplete	Validation activity	Insufficient time for validation
		Requirements or design change	Heavy change activity
Will quality be acceptable?	Process operation	Lack of control	Variation in process Adverse trends in process
		Inappropriate process	Inherently low productivity Inherently low quality
	Methods	Defect removal Defect prevention	Ineffective defect removal Not done
Finish within budget?	Resources required	People availability	Not enough resource to complete on schedule

factors can be associated with specific measures to control each, as in Table 9.2. Where a short explanation can be given it is shown in the table; otherwise, a reference is given to a later section in this chapter.

These development activities form part of MORE; the major risk control activities will have been done during CORE, such as changing or tailoring the

Table 9.2. Measures to take for development risk factors

Risk factors	Monitoring method
Systematically low estimates	Track amount of code unit-tested v. plan, over time (see Sec. 9.2).
Inherently low code productivity	Track trend of work units completed v. planned (see Sec. 9.3).
Long learning-curve	There is really no answer to this other than to identify, during the CORE stage, the tools (or skills) that will be used, and to put in place the appropriate training then. The symptoms of a long learning-curve are an initial divergence in the work units completed v. planned (see Sec. 9.3) followed by the lines becoming parallel. The gap between the two represents a slip in the schedule that will have to be retrieved.
Inappropriate tools/ methods	As before, the secret is to identify the right tools at the CORE stage. The use of wrong tools (such as an inappropriate language for the development of an application) will manifest itself as a divergence of trend in the work-units-completed chart (see Sec. 9.3).
Insufficient time for validation	Provide a visual summary of elapsed time between two levels of review (see Sec. 9.4).
Heavy change activity	Plot the actual changes worked on, and those proposed (see Sec. 8.3).
Process variation and trends	Use manufacturing process statistics to show undesirable trends and nonconformances in code units (see Sec. 9.6).
Inherently low productivity	Inappropriate process (such as the use of heavy quality control checks on simple programming units) is yet another reason for low productivity. Using the work-units-completed chart (see above, under 'Inappropriate tools/methods') it is relatively easy to spot the trend; the real managerial challenge is deciding on the reason and correcting it. The CORE part of this book should help in defining an appropriate process.
Inherently low quality	Inappropriate process (such as the use of minimal quality control checks on complex programming units) is the usual reason for poor quality programming units. See Sec. 9.5 for the interpretation of defect removal figures and the identification of lower-than-acceptable quality.
Ineffective defect removal	Interpretation of the DRM figures in terms of removal and injection of errors (see Sec. 9.5).
Defect prevention not done	The defect prevention process (DPP) is a valuable means of preventing common errors from recurring. The fewer errors that are made during development, the fewer there will be left in the product when it goes to the customer. Consider the use of DPP when you are tailoring your process in CORE. DPP involves analysing the causes of errors found at regular points in the development cycle, and putting action plans in place to remove the causes and prevent the errors from recurring. See the bibliography for references to more complete information.
Not enough resource to complete	Plot future resource estimates against actual work completed and future work estimates (see Sec. 9.7).

development process. During MORE, the risks should have been contained to the point that we just need more information to know whether they will materialize or not. Hence this table presents ways of monitoring the risks so that the information can be gained.

9.2   Code growth and low estimates

It is one of the oldest risks of all in software development: that the code estimates should grow, through DCR activity or simply from a growing realization that the job is bigger than at first thought. Not only is it one of the oldest, but it must be one of the commonest. In our experience, it has been a standing joke that all the initial code size estimates should be doubled. 'Joke' is the wrong word—it is a useful rule-of-thumb. There are three project factors that can be juggled (schedule, resource, and function), and in this sort of situation, one (or more) will have to give. In our experience it is usually the amount of function to be delivered that is more flexible than schedule or resource.

The long-term solution is to become much better at estimating. This is easier than it sounds, but it does not happen overnight, and you do need a strong commitment to measurement and analysis. In the short term, an eagle eye kept on the situation should help you to remain in control.

There may be quite valid reasons why code estimates are growing. If there is a lot of change activity forced on the project by imperative circumstances, then the project will have to accommodate. Often, though, a lot of change activity is a sign of sloppy or incomplete specification work early in the project. Whatever the reason, the risk of code growth can be very real and must be carefully monitored. What follows is one way of monitoring the risk which has proved successful for us.

The monitoring method is a compound chart showing planned versus actual code as it is unit tested. (The qualification 'unit tested' is important here, as it represents a completion criterion for code—the chart will have less value if it represents code just written.) It is good for identifying that a component or product is out of control, and is experiencing code growth that it cannot handle. It is also useful for forecasting worst-case end dates in more marginal situations.

9.2.1   Data

The x-axis represents time in weeks. The following data is plotted (as in Fig. 9.1):

- Unit tested (surface chart)
- UT plan (line-chart type)
- Planned size (surface chart)   The planned size is simply the final build size as it varies against time. (This assumes that the final build is the largest.)
- Builds (line-chart with markers only)

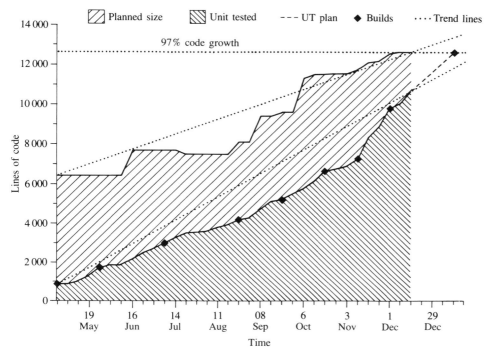

Figure 9.1.   Example of code-growth chart.

There are three further (dotted) lines—two of these showing trends:

- The growth of the planned size of the component
- The production of unit-tested code towards that target

(The two dotted 'trend' lines are simply drawn from size at beginning of the tracked period (both unit-tested size and planned-completion size) to the same figure at the end of the tracked period, i.e., today's date. These lines are extended into the future.) The last dotted line is horizontal and is merely a reference line to mark the current planned size of the component. It is labelled with the percentage growth in planned size since the original component sizing and should be changed whenever the planned code size changes.

9.2.2   *Assumptions*

If code growth is incurred at a faster rate than the code can be written and unit tested then the component is suffering rampant code growth which *must* be reflected in the schedule.

The assumption is also made that the best place from which to draw the trend lines is the first available date, i.e., as coding is beginning and sizing estimates have been produced. Arguments could be advanced for basing the trends on the last few weeks' data, but that is left to the discretion of the user.

9.2.3   *Interpretation*

If the trend lines for tested code and planned code converge, then progress is being made in real terms. A worst-case prognosis might be the date when the two lines cross. If the lines are parallel, then the development team is currently adding DCRs to the code and re-estimating the original work such that they are not getting any closer to finishing it. The lines should *never* diverge!

The corrective action is to exert tighter control on DCRs, or re-examine staffing levels.

9.3   Alternative estimate tracking

The method above assumes that estimates are made in terms of lines of code. A productivity rate is then applied to arrive at task durations. Many planners work directly in terms of person-days to perform a task, and will break a function or work item down into chunks that can be reasonably estimated. Ideally, these will be somewhere between a couple of days and a couple of weeks.

9.3.1   *Data*

When a Gantt chart (bar chart or activity net) is produced for the project, it is possible to construct a table showing the number of tasks that are planned to have been completed at the end of each week. The table can be turned into a chart (see Fig. 9.2) showing the planned task completions over time, on a cumulative basis.

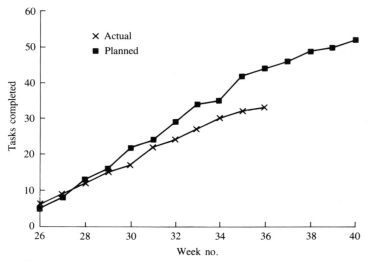

Figure 9.2.   Example of planned v. actual completions.

A line on the chart climbs steadily towards project completion, and makes an excellent visual aid against which to track real progress.

Data should be added weekly. It should be provided by the development team, and should only include those tasks that have been completed. This means those tasks that have actually met their exit criteria, whatever they may be. This avoids the '90 per cent complete' syndrome, and means that you are comparing like with like on your progress chart. The risk within a risk is that people will perform the easy (or small) tasks out of sequence to get an early lift, but clear task labelling and tracking should take care of that.

9.3.2   Interpretation

Analysis of the chart is straightforward. If tasks have been consistently under- or overestimated, then the two lines will diverge. An old and valued principle of estimation is that many small estimates should cancel out the inaccuracies across a large number of units. This is fine if there is no overall bias, in which case the actual line will be roughly coincident with the plan line within a period of four to six weeks. If bias is present, then it will manifest itself in divergence from the plan line over the same period.

The remedial action is to calculate the bias factor from the two gradients of the trend lines, and apply the bias factor to one of the variables: schedule, resource, or function. It is unlikely that a change of productivity can be achieved other than by instituting significant overtime working.

9.4   Inspection schedule prognosis

While everyone (or nearly everyone) agrees that inspection of programming units at the end of each development stage is the best way to ensure the quality of the code, ensuring that the meetings actually take place in an optimum manner is not easy. Getting the right skills together at the right time, so that attendees have enough time to prepare (but development is not held up unduly) demands planning skills of a high order.

The risk is that overoptimistic schedules will be set for the elapsed time between two levels of reviews/inspections (from product level design through to code), because the inspection plan is not based on historical evidence from previous progress on the product. This could mean that the schedules of all dependent stages are exposed.

The terminology that is used below is that used by the originator of the software inspection process, Fagan (1986).

PSR   Product-level design inspection
I0   High-level design inspection
I1   Low-level design inspection
I2   Code inspection

One way to monitor this risk is to provide a summary chart of the elapsed time between two levels of review/inspection for each testable (or inspectable) unit (e.g., line item). The two levels of inspection which can be displayed on this chart are from PSR through to I2. From this it is easy to compare the elapsed time between two levels of inspection for those subcomponents where:

1   Both levels of inspection have been held (e.g., I0 and I1 have been held).
2   Only the earlier inspection has been held (e.g., only the I0 has been held and the I1 is a planned (or forecast) date for that inspection).
3   Neither level of inspection has been held (e.g., both I0 and I1 dates are forecast dates).

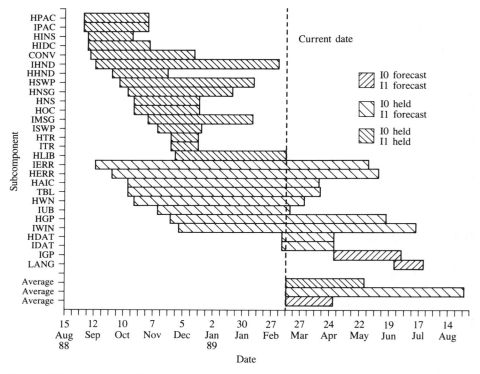

Figure 9.3.   Example of inspection schedule chart.

9.4.1   Data

The chart is a schedule chart (see Fig. 9.3) showing each testable (or inspectable) unit for that component (or other strata of data that shows useful information). For each line item the duration between the inspections is shown by a bar using different hatching for the three categories.

The first data group is used to show the planned or actual start day (from a common reference day) of the first inspection of the pair, e.g., I0. The second, third, and fourth data groups are used to show the timing of the second inspection of the pair, e.g., I1, for the three different categories of inspections pairings mentioned above.

9.4.2 Interpretation

Experience has shown that the scheduling of reviews and inspections is either optimistic or absent and does not reflect what really happened between previous inspections in the same product. From an analysis of average elapsed time between inspections for the inspectable units in each category, it should be possible to predict the probable elapsed time between inspections that have not been held. The predicted times between inspections could be based on best case (e.g., average time for components where both inspections have been held) and worst case (e.g., average time for components where only the first inspection has been held). These times can then be used to predict how long it is going to take to complete the inspection activity. The results of this prediction can then be used to forecast the start of future stages of the project.

Corrective action obviously involves focusing on review/inspection schedule plans to bring them into line with the experience gained from previous projects or from previous history in the current project.

9.5 Error rates at variance with DRM

A common problem encountered during the development stage is that the numbers of defects actually discovered during the defect removal operations do not correspond with the numbers in the plan—the defect removal model (DRM). As a risk, this is a very likely one—but what does it mean for the project?

A certain variation from the plan is tolerable (say 15 per cent) before we need to get concerned. If you find that the actual error rate is 15 per cent more than the expected rate, how should that be interpreted? There are two possibilities: either there are more defects to be found, and a similar proportion of a greater number are being removed; or, the numbers to be found are as expected, but the removal operations are better at removing them than expected. There is, of course, scope for a blurring between these two possibilities.

In the case where the actual numbers are lower than the expected numbers, obviously the inverse of the two possibilities will apply: fewer defects in the first place, or poor defect removal. In each case, one possibility reflects well on the project, and the other badly. Project managers are notoriously optimistic in cases like this: truly a case of the bottle being half full.

In general, you will usually not go far wrong in assuming the worst, but as a risk manager, you will need to confirm your suspicions. The easiest place to start is with the removal of defects. Did the reviews or inspections conform to the standards and procedures laid down for them? Look at the records of the meetings. Were they in session for as long as you would have expected? Were the right people there? Do the records of the meetings show a conscientious approach? If you cannot answer 'yes' to all of these questions, then suspect that the meetings are being skimped, and at best are inefficient and at worst are a waste of time. The remedial action, of course, is to remotivate the review teams: difficult when the pressure is on, but essential if the test phase is not to become out of control.

If the review teams appear to be up to scratch, the next place to look is their incoming material. If the DRM was tracked carefully in previous stages, then the base to the current stage should have been of adequate quality, so look at the complexity, the skills of the people available, the tools that they have available to them, and so on. Try to understand the underlying reasons for the discrepancy. If you can understand the reason, you are more than half-way towards solving the problem, and having the risk under control.

9.6   Process variation and trends

In the introduction to this chapter, the point was made that the significant characteristic of this stage of the development cycle is the process nature of the work. That is, with the same sort of task being carried out over and over again, with the same sort of people and the same sort of tools, the same sort of result (in terms of the qualities we want the finished products to have) should be obtained.

The number of defects made in performing a programming task is not a perfect measure of code quality, but it is a useful indicator of the amount of grief likely to be caused later. If the principle of 'the chain is only as strong as the weakest link' is adopted, then a method for identifying weak links or a trend towards weak links will be very useful.

If we define a process for producing items with measurable criteria (such as defects found in design inspections) then there is a risk that the process will go out of control. (By 'going out of control' we mean that it is not producing all items consistently within certain control limits.) The (almost certain) risk is that reviews/inspections/testing will:

- Uncover numbers of defects that are at variance with the predictions of the quality model
- Be carried out inconsistently across line items

So if our process is likely to go out of control, what is the point of having a process? Because without the process you have not the faintest idea of how out of control you are. (Ring any bells with projects from the past?) With a process in place, at least you can spot what is wrong and do something about it.

To monitor the risk of the process going out of control, we must track the defects arising from reviews/inspections, using statistical quality control (SQC) techniques (from the manufacturing industry) to determine whether or not any particular review/inspection is out of line. SQC charts show normal process capability and flag statistically significant exceptions so corrective action can be taken. It answers the following questions:

- Is the process under control?
- Is the mean value of the items being produced by the process within an acceptable proximity to the predicted value?
- What is the quality of like units over time?

9.6.1 Data

An SQC chart (Fig. 9.4) is a combined scatter plot and line graph showing defects detected by product component. Defect rates are individually plotted as a time series, along the horizontal axis. Control lines, derived from the data for *all* components indicate upper/lower warning and action lines at two and three standard deviations, respectively, from the mean. The mean of the defect rates of the data items is also plotted, with the mean from the DRM, for reference.

Each time new data is generated (e.g., code is inspected) the quality value (e.g., defects/KLOC) and the new mean are replotted for the whole set of components. The new actions and warning lines are plotted from the revised standard deviation.

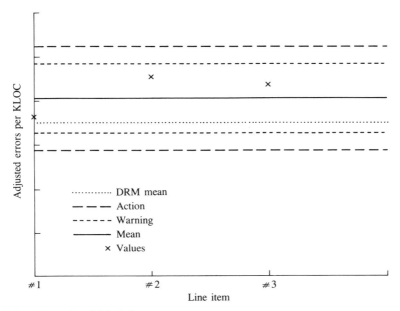

Figure 9.4. Example of SQC chart.

9.6.2   Assumptions

The main assumption is that, because the units being produced are not of a uniform size, some factor can be used to normalize the data. This situation is frequently encountered in the manufacturing industry, and algorithms have been derived to handle it. Any good text on quality control will give the formula for normalizing to size, and it can be programmed into a spreadsheet very easily.

9.6.3   Interpretation

If certain inspections show a defects/KLOC figure outside the action lines then that inspection and design should be reviewed to see why this happened. It may be necessary to repeat a review/inspection, or to justify out-of-line situations: for example, was it a complex design done by inexperienced developers? In such a case the manager may decide to allocate an experienced person to help.

SQC-chart type of analysis could also be used towards the end of a testing phase to identify error-prone modules for investigation or further testing. As an example, when one of the mainframe products that we are familiar with was tracked through the DRM, it was found that the design error rates were slightly, though not significantly, lower than the rate expected. When all of the individual data were analysed using an SQC chart, it was found that all of the components fell within acceptable bounds, except an environment component, which had a very low error rate. When this was investigated, it was found that work was being done on an operating system interface, and the designer for that component had a relatively low skill level in that operating system. Even worse, the people in the inspection had virtually no knowledge of that environment whatsoever.

It seemed fairly likely that the low error rate was more probably due to a low error detection rate, rather than high-quality work. The solution was to import an expert and rehold the inspections. The result, of course, was that the number of errors discovered shot up. This tilted the balance of the DRM the other way—still an anomaly, but one which could now be satisfactorily explained.

9.7   Not enough resource to complete on schedule

When trying to juggle schedule, function and quality, it is all too easy to forget cost in terms of the people required to do the job. Often there is a fixed amount of resource, and to go beyond that resource will extend the cost (budget) of the project unacceptably. Thus there is a risk that the resource required to complete a design, code and unit test (DCUT) event on schedule may be greater than resource available, causing the budget to be exposed.

To monitor this risk, we would like to be able to demonstrate graphically whether the resource is available to complete a series of events on schedule.

9.7.1 Data

The graph is plotted as a time series (Fig. 9.5) where: time is plotted along the *x*-axis; the estimate of work still required is plotted as a bar chart below the *x*-axis; work completed is seen as a bar chart above the *x*-axis; and future resource capacity estimates over time can be seen as a series of lines below the *x*-axis.

9.7.2 Assumptions

The following assumptions are made:

- Effort can be measured in person-days (PDs).
- A PD of effort is a fixed unit of measurement which is not distorted by the type of work being done, whether the effort is spent coding, unit testing, working on new code or working on reused code.
- Calculation of future capacity assumes each person works a five-day week.
- Any allowance for holidays, education, meetings, etc., is already built in to effort-required estimates.

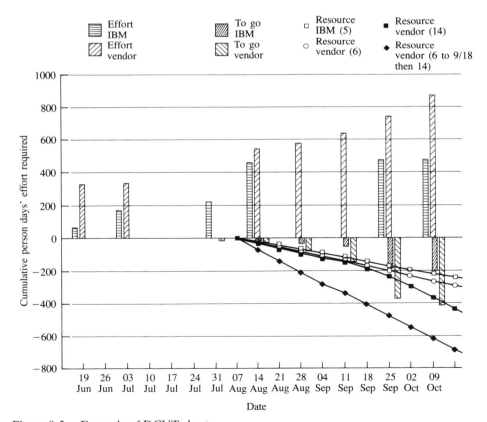

Figure 9.5. Example of DCUT chart.

9.7.3   *Interpretation*

Compare the work still to do with capacity to do it. This will tell you whether the plan is still achievable. Also, the event may still be achievable, but a week-on-week pattern may show the risk is increasing (or decreasing).

If cost really is the main constraint, then corrective action will, in the last analysis, probably involve cutting out function. Before that, consider:

- Reordering the sequence of plan events to optimize spare capacity
- Modifying test plans to reflect DCUT progress

10
Verification

10.1 Of bugs and roosting chickens

The verification stage is the last part of the development cycle before the product is nervously tried out on the customers. It is the stage when all the chickens that escaped flapping their wings during the earlier stages come home to roost. It is the time when any weakness in estimating or controlling the project becomes more and more apparent.

Traditionally, all project dates would be met (albeit with significantly increasing degrees of desperation) until the test stages. The test starts on time, although with only part of the function that was committed, and then the fun begins. A test case is run, an error is found that stops further testing in that area, and the error is passed back to the programmer, who is still trying to finish code for the function that is still undelivered. An impasse is rapidly reached, with testers unable to test an increasing amount of their function because of the backlog of unfixed defects, while the programmers are busy adding to the backlog of untestable code. The test schedule then stretches out to several times its original planned length and all concerned burn gallons of midnight oil to catch up.

In an ideal world, the guidelines in the preceding chapters will have been followed, allowing the project manager to let a smug smile play on his lips while the test team go through the mere formality of demonstrating that the product performs according to specification, before delivering on (or ahead of) schedule, to a delighted customer. As yet, we do not all have our visas to this perfect world, and there is still need to test the final quality *into* the product, by removing those errors that escaped our earlier defect removals, but were not prevalent enough to have triggered the defect prevention process.

There are risks of course in any such process, because of the unknowns involved: we do not know for certain, how many defects still remain to be found, nor do we know for certain what degree of coverage our testing achieves (although there are estimates that can be made).

Using the risk factors table approach (Tables 10.1 and 10.2), the risks can be identified.

Table 10.1. Risk factors in software development

Primary questions	Secondary factors	Tertiary factors	Risk factors
Schedule	Test progress	Quality of code	Error-prone modules Inherently buggy code
		Low bug fix-rate	Programmer availability Backlog of fixes Complexity of code
		Unrealistic plans	Test productivity Schedule too short
Quality	Test effectiveness	Test coverage	Narrow view of testers Missing test cases Defects remaining
		Customer view not tested	Usability Performance Documentation

10.2 Error-prone modules

Rarely will defects be found homogeneously spread through a piece of software. More usually they will tend to cluster in certain parts. Those modules in which higher than average error rates occur are called *error-prone modules*. Their detection is important if the integrity of the whole program is not to be at risk. Once they are detected, then appropriate test plans can be made to exercise them enough to test some quality into them.

Error-prone modules can arise for a variety of reasons—complex function, poor design, volatile requirements—but whatever the reason, they are all characterized by a higher than average error rate *throughout the development cycle*. It is tempting to think that high error rates before validation will lead to low error rates by the end of the cycle, but this is not usually true. Generally, the same proportion of errors are found throughout the product, but the error-prone modules have more to find, and hence there are more errors left in them.

To identify the risk of error-prone modules in a software product, you must highlight their out-of-line behaviour. This is most easily done with *polar charts*. These are sometimes called radar charts or star charts, but the principle is the same: a radius represents the performance at a particular stage, and the compass points represent the different stages (Fig. 10.1).

10.2.1 Data

Each axis of the chart represents a different stage in the development process. (Here, PDR is product design review; I0, I1, I2 represent high-level design, low-level design, and code respectively; and FVT and PVT are function and product verification tests.) A unit distance along the axis represents the average defect density (defects/KLOC) for the product as a whole. The actual defect density is then plotted on the same axis for the subject component.

Table 10.2. Measures to take for validation risk factors

Risk factors	Monitoring methods
Error-prone modules	Identify error-prone modules by diagramming (see Sec. 10.2), and increase testing coverage in those areas.
Inherently buggy code	Predict number of errors expected (see Sec. 10.3), and plan for coverage for fixing by programmers.
Low programmer availability	Prioritize defects in terms of impact on testing; monitor time spent on new code development versus bug fixing by the use of activity codes.
Backlog of fixes	Monitor status of problems found, charting numbers in each state at the end of each reporting period (see Sec. 10.4).
High code complexity	If the program is complex then track complexity of the programming units with one of the complexity measures, such as Halstead or Cyclomatic numbers. Commercial programs are available to make these measurements. Redesign or split high-complexity modules.
Low test productivity	Assign weighting values (points) to the test cases in the test plan, and plan and track test progress based on a test points productivity rate. The points assigned to each test case should represent the coverage and/or the significance of the case. Tracking points completed gives a much better idea of progress than simply tracking cases completed, when trivial cases can distort the picture.
Test schedule too short	Track progress of test cases completed versus time, and predict remaining schedule using the 70/50 rule (see Sec. 10.5).
Narrow view of testers	Involve users (or specialists in the application) in the test team, if the testers have a limited view of the subject.
Missing test cases	If it is suspected that the test plan may not provide good test coverage, then employ one of the commercially available test coverage monitoring programs. These provide statistical reports on the line-by-line execution of program statements, and allow tuning of test cases to improve coverage.
Defects remaining	Predict remaining defects from test results (see Sec. 10.6).
Poor usability	It is one of those unfortunate facts of life that if testers find usability problems, it is usually too late to do anything about it. If usability is an important quality characteristic (and it always is) then plan for it from the earliest stages: involve the users in prototyping exercises to make sure that you have got it right at the design stage.
Poor performance	As for usability. Testers can measure that performance targets are being achieved, but it is very difficult to improve poor performance at this stage. If performance is critical, then achieving it should be made the subject of a performance plan, and performance modelling should be done at the design stages.
Inadequate documentation	User-oriented documentation can be corrected at this stage, though usually not redesigned. If there is a risk that the documentation will not be acceptable, then prepare a DRM in the same way as for programming defects, and track documentation defects. Involve writers early if defects discovered exceed the plan.

A unit circle is drawn representing the performance of a hypothetical average item through these stages. Another polygon is drawn representing the performance of the subject.

There is a practical consideration to take into account here. If there is a large number of modules then it is obviously impractical to plot them all. There will

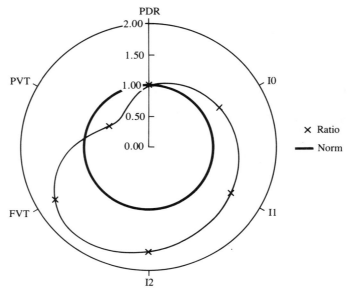

Figure 10.1.   Example of polar chart.

usually be some way of aggregating them by function or requirement item that represents a sensible logical grouping of modules sharing the same characteristics. This will cut down the plotting considerably, but will still give enough granularity for the testers to home in on the neediest areas.

10.2.2 Interpretation

For an error-prone module, the polygon will be well outside the unit circle representing the average performance. A reliable module will lie wholly inside.

If you have the courage of your convictions (which means that you believe that the defect data plotted represents good defect removal practices from the previous stages) then the testers need give only cursory attention to the reliable components. This will have to be counterbalanced by extra attention to those components that show a polygon substantially outside the unit circle. Effectively, better use will be made of test time, and the risk of the product being released to users with unreliable areas within it is significantly reduced.

10.3   Predicting test discovery rates

One of the characteristics of a project under schedule pressure is that parts of the process can be skimped—and the parts that are skimped are invariably those that relate to defect removal or defect prevention. The risk that is addressed here is that the number of defects found after unit test will stretch the test period out with additional testing, either because you are not finding the problems that you expected (poor test design?), or because you keep finding more problems, as you test more deeply (poor code quality?). Or you might just have a poorly calibrated DRM. What we would like to do is to monitor the discovery rate of problems against what we expect.

10.3.1 Data

The 'what we expect' should be easy. The delivery of function to the test should be defined in the test plan with the code size of each piece of function. The quality plan will contain the DRM(s), so that the predicted defects in each delivery of code is found by multiplying code size by the DRM error rate for the test. The cumulative number of defects to be found can then be plotted over time. This assumes an homogeneous distribution of defects. If this assumption seems to be grossly untrue, then the polar charts from Sec. 10.2 should give an indication of how to recalculate.

Tracking is done on a regular basis: fortnightly seems to work best for large projects. Tracking is most effectively done by charting. An example chart is shown in Fig. 10.2. The data that needs to be collected is the number of problems that have been raised in the last time period. This number needs to be converted to actual test problems—the problems raised will probably contain problems raised elsewhere, and invalid problems.

To plot real test problems, an approximation is involved. As the test proceeds, problems raised earlier will be discovered to be either valid or invalid, and will be recorded as such in the problem log. For the purposes of the analysis, we need to know the current ratio of valid/total test problems. This ratio (which we have found to be typically 0.6) needs to be applied to all of the problems that have been raised but are, as yet, unresolved. Thus a computed value of valid test problems can be plotted against the predicted value for the current time.

10.3.2 Interpretation

The trend apparent between the predicted value and the computer valid FV problems should help decide whether extra testing is likely or more development effort for problem fixing should be scheduled. The predictive power of the chart can be increased by extending the line of actual data with an estimate of the future discovery rate of problems by the test team. Again, history is of help here, but our own experience indicates that a problem raising rate of two per tester/week is appropriate during the earlier stages of testing, rising to six per tester/week as the product becomes usable and fully testable.

10.4 Tracking the backlog of test errors

Because of the volumes that are usually found, the fixing of defects should be under process control, but rarely is. The problem is that two effects are working

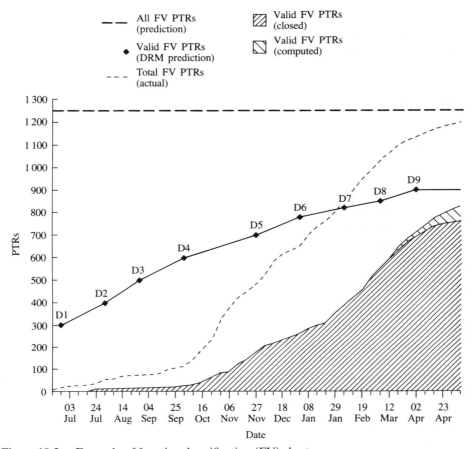

Figure 10.2.   Example of functional verification (FV) chart.

counter to each other: the time at which defects are being found in greatest numbers—early in the test—is when the programmers are usually least able to work on them. Thus it should not be too surprising to see a backlog of defects mounting up. The risk, however, is that the backlog becomes unmanageable (the testers cannot continue testing, or the programmers cannot finish their development).

To monitor the risk of an unmanageable backlog, we need to be able to categorize the status of the defect—the point that it has reached in the fixing process. With minor variations, the following states are usually used:

1   Raised (problem is recorded in the log)
2   Answered (problem is acknowledged as a defect—or not)
3   Fixed (defect has been corrected and tested by fixer)
4   Complete (defect has been regression-tested by test team, or acknowledged as not a real defect).

10.4.1 Data

At any one time, the sum of all the problems will be represented by four subtotals of the different states, which can be plotted as components of a bar in a bar chart. The data should be collected from the defect recording system (problem log), which should be a repository for all defects raised, and their subsequent history. The objective of the chart is to show how many problems are waiting to be handled by both development and test. It is also used to show the actual problem raising, fixing, and closing numbers in a week. Lines represent the current problem backlogs (total problems waiting for a fix, and in-fixtest) and bars show the actual raised, fixed, and closed in each time period (see Fig. 10.3).

10.4.2 Interpretation

The shape of the graph shown in Fig. 10.3 is typical, and illustrates the problems waiting-for-fix falling to meet the rising problems in-fixtest. This should be marked by large numbers of problems being resolved. When raising rates are still

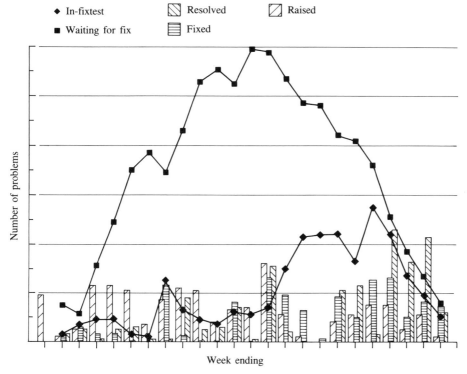

Figure 10.3.   Example of test backlog chart.

high well into the test, and the shape of the chart differs markedly from that shown here, analyse the raising and fixing rates to find the extent of the problem.

10.5   Test schedule too short

Counting the 'successful' completion of a test case (by which we mean running to the end, producing the predicted results) is a useful way of tracking progress in a test. Unfortunately, initial results tend to be too optimistic, for the initial heady progress tends to slow towards the end.

The risk of the test schedule being too short can be monitored by the use of a rule of thumb that has proved successful in our own environment. It is a matter of empirical observation, based on many tests, that a system test will be approximately half-way through (in elapsed time) when 70 per cent of the test cases have completed successfully. (Factors which tend to change productivity, like learning curves, and more difficult problems being found later, are built in to this empirical observation.) This rule appears to work well for most tests, though some observers claim that for the earlier functional verification test (FVT), a 60/50 rule fits better.

Tracking can be as simple or as complicated as you like. We tend to use a chart similar to Fig. 10.4 to fit a 70/50 curve to the available data, so that a projection can

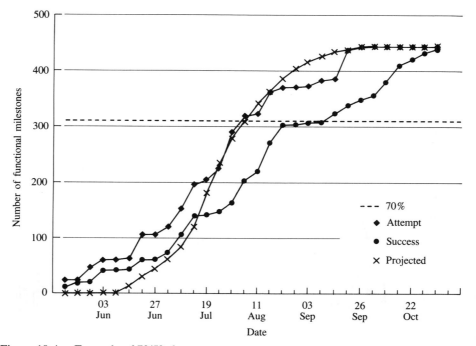

Figure 10.4.   Example of 70/50 chart.

be made early in the test. This sort of projection, of course, carries its own risks, but it has proved useful, and reasonably reliable.

10.5.1 Data

A line graph should be plotted with some, or all, of the following types of data against time on the x-axis:

- Test cases (or equivalent) planned to be completed.
- Test cases (or equivalent) attempted so far.
- Test cases (or equivalent) successfully completed.
- Test cases (or equivalent) projected by 70/50 model. It may be safest to project two lines: a best case, and worst case.

A 70 per cent reference line may also be shown.

10.5.2 Assumptions

The fundamental assumption here is that test progress is nonlinear, and is best described by 70 per cent success in 50 per cent of the time. Intuitively, this is a reasonable model, as the easier test cases will be disposed of quickly, and those with the more intractable or pervasive problems will naturally tend to be completed last. The only question is whether the suggested proportions are right for your establishment. Your historical data should provide you with some reference points of your own.

Note also that it is assumed that test effort is applied consistently throughout the duration of the test.

10.5.3 Interpretation

The interpretation of the chart will depend on how much confidence you have in your curve fitting, which will, in turn, depend on how far through the test you are. If the risk of overrunning the test schedule appears to be a real one, then consider the following actions:

- Analyse outstanding problems to see if there are any critical ones blocking progress in significant areas.
- Examine test matrices in conjunction with error-prone component analysis (see Sec. 10.2) to see if stable components can have reduced testing.
- Look at the effect of overlapping test schedules.
- Try causal analysis on the most disruptive problems to see if they can be prevented from delaying testing in the future.

10.6   Predicting defects remaining at the end of testing

Exactly how good is the product after it finishes testing and is it ready for delivery to the customer? This is the sort of question that can never be satisfactorily answered, because of the many dimensions of quality and their often subjective nature. However, there is one characteristic of the product that is of immediate concern to the customers, and which will profoundly influence their view of it. This is the degree of 'bugginess' that they experience. If a program works, and gives the right answers unfailingly, then shortcomings in usability or performance may be grumbled over, but probably will not produce the unreasoning rage that programming errors will.

On the assumption, then, that your testing will not produce a completely error-free product, what is the risk of delivering a program with an unacceptable number of errors in it? This is a question that has had some interesting mathematical techniques applied to it, usually based on fitting curves to error-detection profiles through the development cycle, and usually giving an answer with a confidence range so wide as to be useless. What is described here is a far simpler approach, that does not use any complicated mathematics, and gives a confidence range as narrow (or as wide) as your experience dictates. It has worked well for us in a number of different situations, in a location where we have accumulated enough experience to apply confidently the judgements needed.

Consider the final test performed on a product before it is given to the customer. The test will find a number of problems, which will be faithfully recorded in a problem log (won't they?) with details of who/when found, severity, status, and so on. The product is then handed on to the customer(s) who, in the normal course of events, will find some more problems: rather fewer than found in the test, we hope. These too will be recorded in a log, so that we can look back at any program or product and see how many problems were found by the last test, and how many by the user before it became stable. (There may well be problems that are still lurking in the code, unfound by the users, but as they have not caused anyone a problem, we can be forgiven for ignoring them in this analysis.)

For a typical program we have two numbers: the errors found during the test and after it. Adding them together, we have the total number of errors available to be found; by dividing the number found by the test by the total, we have a measure of *test effectiveness*. This is usually known as the *defect removal effectiveness* (DRE):

$$\text{Defect removal effectiveness} = \frac{\text{Number of defects found in test}}{\text{Number of defects present at test start}}$$

If we look at this number for several different programs, we can start to get a good idea of just how effective we are at removing errors in that test. In our experience, that figure will usually be in the range 65–70 per cent for the sort of system software that we are familiar with. (This range relates to our own processes, and our rather aggressive quality targets. Other sources quote typical figures nearer to 50 per cent.)

Of course, if we know the effectiveness of our test, then we know how many errors are left in the product, and hence when we can stop testing. There are ways in which this figure can be estimated, such as by seeding known errors into the code, and seeing what proportion are found by the test team, but to get a statistically meaningful answer from this method, a lot of work has to be expended in setting up realistic data, and in most circumstances this is not justified. You could also look back at the history of your past test experience, and look for patterns in your test effectiveness so that you can make a good guess at what you have achieved this time, based on parameters such as complexity, size, test effort, etc.

However, it would only be a guess, albeit an educated guess. This can be improved by using extra data available to you from the previous test(s). Remember the analysis of test effectiveness—that can be extended back for as many test stages as you have data. For the next test back, we know how many errors left it to go into the last test; we know how many errors it discovered; so we can calculate the test effectiveness in the same way as before. Again, this sort of analysis is only for understanding the sort of performance that has been achieved in the past, but it will help to make sense of the data that is collected from the current program.

Now, let us assume that we have two sets of data from the two last tests conducted on the product, and we want to know if it has reached an acceptable figure of 1 (or less) defects left in it in each 1000 lines of code (KLOC). In the last test (ZT) 1.51 defects/KLOC were found, and in the previous test (YT), 3.21 were found, making 4.72 in total found by the last two tests. We do not know exactly how many defects are left in the product, but our objective is for less than 1 defect/KLOC. (In this example, all data values have been normalized to give a target value of unity. In the original example, the target value was an awkward fractional value.)

Let us assume for one moment that there are 6 defects in total at the start of YT. That means that YT removes defects with an effectiveness of 3.21/6, or about 54 per cent. It also means that $(6 - 3.21)$ or 2.79 defects go forwards to ZT, which therefore has an effectiveness of 1.51/2.79, or 54 per cent again: 1.28 defects/KLOC are left to be found by the users.

If we did the same sort of calculations with a new starting value, say 5.5, we would come up with a new pair of DREs (58 and 66 per cent) and a smaller number of defects left, 0.78 in each KLOC. Given the test data that we have collected, for each possible number of defects left in the product, there is a unique pair of DREs associated with the two tests. Table 10.3 gives a typical set of calculations.

The figures of Table 10.3 are best plotted on a chart as in Fig. 10.5. A horizontal line drawn through the y-axis gives the remaining defects left for any (unique) pair of DREs. Note that the intersection of the two curves has no significance other than as an arithmetic coincidence. The trick is to decide which pair of DREs is

Table 10.3. Calculate paired DREs and residual defects

Starting defects	6.2	6.0	5.8	5.6	5.4	5.2	5.0	4.8
	YT removes 3.21 defects/KLOC							
YT DRE (%)	51.7	53.5	55.3	57.3	59.4	61.7	64.2	66.8
Defects to ZT	2.99	2.79	2.59	2.39	2.19	1.99	1.79	1.59
	ZT removes 1.51 defects/KLOC							
ZT DRE (%)	50.5	54.1	58.3	63.2	69.0	75.9	84.4	95.0
Defects to customer	1.48	1.28	1.08	0.88	0.68	0.48	0.28	0.08

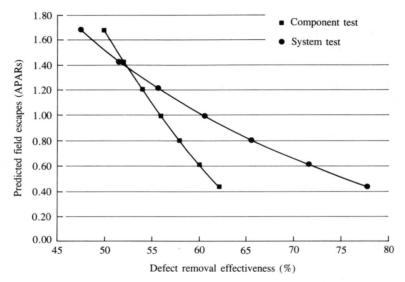

Figure 10.5.   Varying relationship of paired DREs.

most likely. Selecting any one value of a DRE is difficult, as we saw earlier, but the fact that *both* DREs have to be likely limits the choice considerably, as one figure changes much more rapidly than the other.

Suppose that, after considering all the evidence (see later), the probabilities of the different DREs were assessed in Tables 10.4 and 10.5. If the two DREs were independent of each other, then the most likely combination would be a ZT DRE centred on 68 per cent together with a YT DRE centred on 55 per cent. However, Fig. 10.6 shows that these two ranges do not coincide with DRE values that would be considered high for both tests. Therefore a compromise position has to be taken: between the two plotted ranges there is an area for which both tests have medium probability, and it is here that DRE pairings have the the greatest combined probability. Therefore, the most likely value is chosen from this intermediate range.

Table 10.4. Estimated probabilities for YT

DRE range (%)	Estimated probability
50–52	Low
52–54	Medium
54–56	High
56–58	Medium
58–60	Low
60–62	Low
62–64	Very low

Table 10.5. Estimated probabilities for ZT

DRE range (%)	Estimated probability
50–54	Very low
54–58	Very low
58–62	Low
62–66	Medium
66–70	High
60–74	Medium
74–78	Low
78–82	Very low

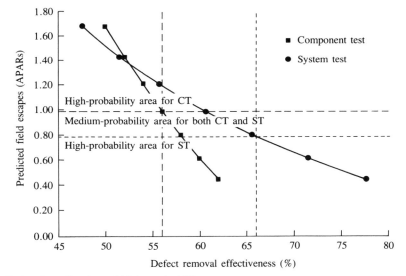

Figure 10.6. Localization of high-probability areas.

The key to the interpretation of the chart lies in the judgement that is applied to the probabilities in the DREs.

10.6.1 *Judgement*

In general, it is not possible to make absolute estimates of the DRE of a test; estimates will be relative to previous or similar experience. Ideally, there will be data from a previous release of the same product from which an estimate can be derived. Alternatively, experience with similar products can be utilized, or even the experience of the test team on dissimilar products. A starting point is needed which is then modified by the changed factors in the product being evaluated.

Table 10.6.   Test factors affecting DRE

Test factor	Metric
Size of product	Thousands of lines of new/changed code (KLOC)
Test planning time	Person-weeks (PWs) per KLOC
Test execution time	PW/KLOC
Number of unique test-cases	Test cases/KLOC
Experience of test team	High/medium/low
Specific product expertise in team	High/medium/low
Duration of test	Weeks
Complexity of function	High/medium/low
Machine time spent testing	Machine hours/KLOC

The factors listed in Table 10.6 are all significant for the DRE of a test. Obviously not all of these factors will be suitable for all products, indeed some of the factors duplicate others to some extent. A subset of three or four factors, supported by reliable data from a comparison product and the assessed product, should be sufficient.

In this example, the complete defect history for the previous release, release n, was not available, but with more than a year's data gathered, the product was consistently within its defect forecasts, and appeared to have a strong probability of meeting its defect target of 1 defect/KLOC. By making the assumption that this would be its final field quality, it was possible to calculate the DREs for the release 1 tests, and these were 56 per cent for YT, and 65 per cent for ZT.

The claims for improvement in the tests over release n were quite significant. For release$(n + 1)$YT:

- A high degree of vitality in the test team
- Application specialists brought in to increase expertise
- Greater proportional effort (>3 PW/KLOC) than is seen in most comparable size products

Similar points were made for ZT:

- Parallel test carried out on two sites
- Fresh test cases written by application specialists brought in
- Significant proportional effort of >5 PW/KLOC

In the final analysis, incorporating the experience and judgement of the people involved, the range between the two high-probability areas for the two tests was 0.78–0.99 field escapes/KLOC (where field escapes are those defects that get through the testing process to be shipped with the product that is distributed to the customer). Rather than choose the middle of the range, greater credibility was attached to the ZT data, because more subjective factors had biased the YT assessment downwards. Choosing a final most-likely value of 0.8 field escapes/KLOC meant that the YT DRE had to float up from the original high-probability

54–56 per cent to 58 per cent, while very little adjustment was needed for ZT: the final value was 65.5 per cent, from a high probability range of 66–70 per cent.

The final step in the interpretation of the chart was to decide what the maximum likely number of field escapes would be. This is equivalent to giving a confidence range for statistical sampling of hardware measurements. Whereas one could calculate a 99 per cent confidence range for true statistical samples, here one can only decide the minimum DREs that can be contemplated; in this particular case, it was decided that under no circumstances could ZT have a DRE of less than 56 per cent. This figure was derived from analysis of DREs from many ZTs, which indicated that for this type of product a DRE of less than 60 per cent is rare, with a minimum recorded of 56 per cent. This enabled a statement to be made (using pseudo-statistical language) to the effect that: 'there is a 99 per cent probability that the field escapes will be less than 1.2 defects/KLOC'.

10.6.2 *Considerations for use*

The following are worth bearing in mind when making an assessment using this method.

1   Understanding of the development process

Although the method described is exclusively concerned with test data, knowledge of the earlier development process should not be overlooked. Data from (for instance) design inspections or specification reviews can give valuable insight into the quality (or otherwise) of the process that gave rise to the product being assessed, and may help to understand the significance of unexpectedly high or low figures.

2   Crossover point on the graph

The crossover point on the graph has no significance, other than to indicate the probable left-hand margin of the working range of DREs. Experience and theory both indicate that a higher DRE will be obtained on the later test rather than the earlier, which means that it is probable that the final pairing should lie to the right of the intersection.

3   Relationship of field escapes to defects

The term 'field escapes' has been used to refer to the number of defects that the test process fails to remove from the product. There is no reason to believe, of course, that all these escapes will necessarily be found as defects (reported by customers), so the final defect figure could be better than a theoretical field escape figure. However, when previous experience is drawn upon to guide the choice of

DREs (strongly recommended, as above) then the (unknown) relationship between defects and field escapes is automatically taken into account. The stronger the relationship between the product being assessed and the calibrating product, the more accurate the final result is likely to be.

4   Extensions to use

There is no reason why the method need only be used exactly in the way described. If the data is available, even more precision and confidence can be obtained by using three or more tests. The method can also be used to assist in test planning by:

- Using the method as described, but earlier in the process, or
- Using the data from one test only, and making assumptions about the DRE of the next test.

Enough information has been given above for readers to be able to make the necessary adjustments for themselves.

11
Delivery (announce and ship)

11.1 The final hurdle?

With the test phases successfully negotiated, all that now remains is to tell the world about the product and wait for them to beat a path to your door. Telling the world is the activity of *Announcement*. This may be a large set-piece presentation, or a small advertisement in the trade press; it may be a notice on an electronic bulletin board seen only by members of your company, or the subject of an international press release which shoots around the globe in a matter of seconds. *Shipment* is a case of giving the world what you told the world it would get. It is a matter of ensuring that if Joe Public goes into his local Computa-Store at 0900 on the day your advertisement said that release 73.4 of your best selling game program 'InterGalactic WipeOut for Windows' would be generally available then there, sitting on the shelves, will be that very product.

Announcement, followed by shipment—at this stage there should not be any risks, should there?

This is mostly true. If a product ship is a risky exercise then something has gone badly wrong earlier, be it through poor planning, or poor execution of a good plan. Even so, there are some risks associated with this stage. While they are usually the primary concern of other areas of the product team, such as marketing, the development organization does have a part to play in helping to ensure that this final phase proceeds smoothly.

Using the risk factors table approach once again, the risks might be identified as in Table 11.1. These risk factors can be associated with a specific measure to control each, as in Table 11.2. Where a short explanation can be given it is shown in the table; otherwise a reference is given to a later section in this chapter.

11.2 Quality certification

Quality certification, as the term implies, is the activity of ensuring that a product has met its stated commitments in terms of quality, where quality, as we have said numerous times in this text, includes at least the attributes of capability, usability,

Table 11.1. Risk factors in delivery

Primary questions	Secondary factors	Tertiary factors	Risk factors
Is it safe to announce the product?	Timing	Current status	Announce a date that will not be met
	Details	Content/quality	Promise, but do not deliver
			Deliver, but did not promise
Is it safe to ship the product?	Content and quality	CUPRIMD factors	Unsatisfactory content and/or quality
	Acceptability	Customer perception	Do not like the product
		Service levels	Poor response to problems

performance, reliability, installability, maintainability and documentation. In theory, quality certification should be a nonevent. If the approaches outlined in this book have been followed—particularly those of Chapter 4 regarding the production of a quality plan and the subsequent tracking of the items covered by that plan—then quality risks will have been spotted and addressed throughout development. The quality of the product must be good, yes?

No, not always. At least, not entirely. In practice, the business of quality certification is about rather more than simply nailing those products that have chosen to ignore quality considerations totally; it is a valid exercise, even if every quality plan commitment has been fulfilled in its entirety.

11.2.1 *Quality certification objectives*

Quality certification has the following objectives:

1   To assess objectively the quality of the product before it is formally exposed to customers or potential customers. That is, we are conducting one final piece of risk management with a quality certification—that of minimizing the risks of a loss of goodwill, or of a damaged reputation, through either releasing, or even announcing, an unsuitable product.

   This last point is important. Announcement, in its way, can be as much an exposure of the product as shipment. Customers may well base their IT plans on the strength of your announcement. Quality certification at announce time is a safety check that they will see what they are told they will see.

2   To ensure, before both announce and ship, that all required quality activities are complete—or can confidently be expected to be complete—and that plans are in place for the follow-on activities required. The real business world may dictate that a product be announced at an earlier point in the development cycle than would otherwise be chosen. (The same should never be said about ship!). If this is the case, then quality certification is the activity through which

Table 11.2. Dealing with delivery risk factors

Risk factor	Action plan constituents
Announce a date that will not be met	A key element of the announcement of a software product is its projected availability date. The risk we run is in announcing a date and failing to meet it—a risk that can *only* manifest itself through poor project tracking and a lack of information. An obvious, if unadventurous, way of reducing this risk to nothing is to announce and ship on the same day. Of course, this loses the advantage to be gained of giving early warning to your customers so that they prepare to install your product on day one. The best way is to know your product's status and, thereby, announce a date that you know there is little risk you will fail to meet.
Promise, but do not deliver	In terms of content and quality, this is similar to the above. An announcement should contain details of what the product will be offering, and—in areas like usability and performance—may promise some level of quality. If quality tracking is poor, or nonexistent, then this part of the announcement will be at risk. Delivering a product with less in it than the customer expected is not a good way of enhancing a reputation.
Deliver, but did not promise	Not so much a disaster, more a missed opportunity. Poor status tracking may mean that at announce time you err on the side of caution and only announce features of the product which you can actually see—even though, with the right level of confidence, it would be possible to make a greater impact on the market with a fuller announcement. In each of the above, using the techniques outlined in the previous chapters will reduce the risk of approaching an announcement without adequate status information.
Unsatisfactory content and/or quality	Is this likely? After tackling the risks inherent in software specification, and after measuring and tracking all of the CUPRIMD elements of software quality, the answer should be 'no'. To be absolutely certain, plan to conduct formal quality certification exercises prior to both announce and availability (see Sec. 11.2).
Do not like the product	Again, this should be so unlikely as to be not worth bothering about. A programme of customer involvement from requirements onwards should have reduced this risk to negligible proportions.
Poor response to problems	Users will have problems. As such, they present a risk to the software developer which is rather subtle. The reason for this is that the risk tends not to be that—unless it causes a catastrophe or has an average MTTF of less than a minute—the software will be seen to be bad *per se*. It is more that an organization which cannot respond satisfactorily to user problems faces the risk of a diminished reputation in the eyes of its customers: insidious, and very costly. Adequate customer support is crucial (see Sec. 11.3).

we can verify that the likelihood—and thereby the risk—of shipping a poor-quality product is at an acceptable level.

3   To ensure that action plans are put in place where objectives are not being met. Quality certification is a binary go/no go exercise. If quality targets have not been met, then that fact can be either:

(a)   Accepted as legitimate (for whatever reasons) and the risk borne; in other words, the product is granted a quality deviation in some respect, or

(b) Not accepted—in such cases it would be the objective of the certification review to ensure that plans have been put in place to address the delinquent areas, and to ensure, also, that the product is not announced/ shipped until they are addressed!

11.2.2 The certification process

The key points about the certification process are:

1 The product owner is responsible for the preparation and presentation of the certification package (see Sec. 11.2.3). These responsibilities may be delegated but the product owner must have reviewed and concurred with the certification package.
2 The presentation should be made by a person who is empowered to resolve any issues that might surface during the presentation.
3 Resolution of an issue, or a committed resolution plan must take place before the certification meeting closes.
4 Certification should be scheduled to allow time for rework and issue resolution; otherwise the risk will become a certainty that the product announcement/shipment absolutely must go ahead because there is no time to do the rework.
5 Announcement certification should cover all aspects of the product which are to be included in the announcement. If not everything is to be announced, then this should be stated in the certification package.

11.2.3 Certification presentation content

There really should be no discussion about what is needed for a quality certification presentation—or about where it should come from. In Chapter 4 we discussed at length the role and content of the quality plan. This, we said, should define:

• Quality targets
• Quality techniques
• Quality measures

and, in addition, be a 'living document', that is, a document regularly updated with quality measurements as they were taken.

That having been done, the quality certification package is—no less, and not much more—the current version of the quality plan. Details of techniques followed, measurements taken, and progress against the quality targets form the core of the certification package content. The only additional items needed are likely to be:

• Schedules for remaining activities
• Requests, with supporting justification, for any quality deviations

Based on this information, a certification review board will be well placed to deal with the risk of presenting a poor-quality product to the world.

11.3   Customer support

Finally, we consider briefly the subtle risks inherent in the Cinderella activity of customer support. The risks are subtle because they impinge on such intangibles as reputation and customer goodwill—the first manifestation of which may be a poor score on your next customer satisfaction survey if you are lucky, and no more orders from that particular customer if you are not.

On the face of it, customer support for software products amounts to two activities:

- Offering help and guidance—the help desk
- Fixing bugs—system support

Both are risk areas with, probably and perhaps unexpectedly, the first being the bigger risk area.

11.3.1   The help desk

Users ring a help line because they have a problem, not an error necessarily, but a problem. To the user, that problem is the most important thing in the world at that moment. Leaving aside the few callers who ring a help line and think later, most users will have picked up the phone only after a long period of trial and error, online help scouring and even manual reading. The risk the software developer runs is that a poor or inadequate response to this customer could result in that person's goodwill being scarred for life.

How, then, should a software developer address this risk? Let us take it the other way round. The software developer should *not* address this risk by staffing their help desk with programmers who only started with them the day before yesterday, on the grounds that 'it will help them find their way round our products quickly'. Staffing a help desk with people who actually know about the products they are supposed to be helping their customers with is possibly the single most neglected area of the software development cycle . . . apart, that is, from system support . . .

11.3.2   System support

The classic blunder of allocating new and untried programmers to system support can be dealt with quickly. It is crass, it is a lunatic practice—and apparently it is still being done in some companies.

By definition, the hardest bugs to find and fix are those which escape into the field—if they were easy, they would have been found before then. Putting junior programmers on to this activity (because their seniors are off doing the next, more important, job) is therefore asking for trouble. Why does it continue to happen? Because the 'best' programmers want to be writing new programs, not maintaining old ones. There is no fun in that.

It appears to be an intractable problem. For the project manager, it has to be recognized as a risk.

The other source of trouble in dealing with user problems is that, from the user's point of view, they are not fixed fast enough. The reasons for this become apparent if we consider the phenomenon of 'the problem' from two different points of view.

The developer's view tends to be in system terms:

- Is this problem valid or invalid?
- If valid, is it high severity or low?

Given the answers to these two questions, the average system supporter will aim to deal with high-severity valids as a matter of priority. The fact that a large number of users with a 'minor' problem might be a bigger risk to the software developer's reputation than one user with a big problem is often overlooked.

Consider things from the customer's viewpoint:

- There is no such thing as an invalid problem! All my problems are valid, because they are stopping me from making progress—even if I do not understand how the product works through poor usability, or a lack of documentation.
- I may be able to accept a delay in getting a solution to my problem, so long as I am convinced that somebody understands why it is a problem to *me*—and demonstrates that fact quickly.

Overcoming the risks inherent in system support, then, requires a shift of perspective on the part of the project manager faced with setting up a software support service.

The key objective is often to set up service effort that responds quickly to all problems, recognizing that for the customer, all problems are valid. It is often the case that a strong, positive response to a customer's problem can build greater customer satisfaction than no problems whatsoever.

Secondly, move heaven and earth to staff the service at the technical level necessary. If it is not possible to obtain staff—at least in the early days—who actually developed the product then it is essential that those who are recruited receive adequate training well in advance of their being needed to deal with a customer in anger (perhaps literally).

Part Four
LORE—learning from the optimum risk environment

The Victorian improver, Samuel Smiles, said 'We often discover what *will* do, by finding out what will not do; and probably he who never made a mistake never made a discovery.' This is a good, positive view that encourages risk-taking; but it has to be balanced by its corollary: 'Those who do not learn from their mistakes are doomed to repeat them.'

This part of the book is about ensuring the discoveries are not buried, and the mistakes do not become time-honoured. Just as we mature as individuals through our life experiences, so a project manager can mature through project experience—but project timescales are such that the lessons can be lost or blurred, or buried under an avalanche of other information.

What is needed is a chance to absorb the lessons, to sort out what is worth keeping, and what can be discarded. This is the thinking that develops the models that enhance your management capability. This thinking-through the project afterwards is covered in Chapter 12, while Chapter 13 bridges across to the next time around. Do not pass up the chance of being an even better project manager in your next project!

12
Postship reviews

12.1 Mistakes? Me?

The project is over. Master discs have been cut, publicity and marketing are going to town, the launch programme is scheduled—there is nothing left to do now but bask in a little bit of glory, take a few days' holiday and then dive in to the next project.

True? No. If ever a so-called truism actually turned out to be true it is the one which says, 'we learn from our mistakes'. At this stage of the project, when euphoria is high and back-slapping is the order of the day, we ignore this message at our peril. Learning lessons from what has gone before, capturing those lessons in a way that others can at least examine: if these activities are not undertaken then we have already saddled the followup product with its first risk—the risk that we will go right ahead and make the same mistakes again. Worse, possibly, we may not repeat those things that actually went right!

Be aware of the usual arguments trotted out against conducting a postship review:

- It is not worth the effort, besides we are already starting to think about release 2 . . .

  It is worth the effort. If an outlay of a few person-days results in the quashing of just one high risk then it will be an investment well rewarded.

- The team is being broken up, people are moving on, being promoted . . .

  This is more of an argument for carrying out a postship review quickly than an argument against conducting one at all! If team members are not going to be around in the future, capturing their experience becomes even more important.

- It was not a happy project, so much went wrong. Let it rest in peace. Why rake over the ashes? . . .

  Postship reviews are about capturing experience, not emotions. They are not exercises in apportioning blame but in objectively identifying lessons that should be learnt. The fact that a project went badly wrong means that such lessons are certainly there; it simply compounds the felony not to look for them and learn from them.

- It was a happy project. Everything went right . . .

  So capture the details! Analyse them! Frame them! Whatever happens, do not let them go! There is no law against doing things right a second time.

So, postship reviews are crucial. Development managers might argue about the feasibility of code reuse, but not about its benefits. Why should there be any argument about the benefits of experience reuse?

12.2   Not a project report—an experience report

The obvious way of capturing experience is to get everybody involved in the project—developers, testers, writers, . . . , usually everybody except the project manager—to write a 'project report'. Unfortunately, this is a job with a boredom factor approaching infinity. Nobody does a project report with enthusiasm, except possibly for the section which provides scope for criticizing the performance of the project manager.

What happens then? The reports are collected together, read in one sitting by the project manager (who will only be looking for criticisms of the project manager anyway) then consigned to the archives (especially if they contain criticisms of the project manager). Okay, so it is not quite like that; but it is all too easy for the process to degenerate into something not far removed.

The crucial thing is to ensure from the outset that this is not simply a bureaucratic exercise, but that the reports will be used. In other words, that they form a key element in a process of experience capture. A small, but significant, step in this direction is the choice of name. Forget 'project report'. This implies a blow-by-blow account of what the individual actually did on a daily basis. This is not what is wanted. What we are after is *experience*—so why not talk in terms of an *experience report*?

Next, set out some objectives. Why are people being asked to spend their valuable time writing experience reports?

- To improve the efficiency and effectiveness of all parties involved in product development and support through the application of lessons learned.
- To build up an 'experience database' of reference material.

12.2.1 Structure and content

For some people—curiously, often those most comfortable with a multiplicity of programming languages—writing anything in English is a considerable strain. Make life easy by providing a defined structure to the report:

- Administrative stuff
- Author's project responsibilities
- Lessons learned
- Recommendations

Nothing complicated is needed. What we are after is capturing experience, not adding yet another volume to the shelves of the world's libraries. It might even be a good idea to impose/suggest a maximum length for the report. Even if the writer is happy to churn stuff out by the mile, the reader might not be so happy to read it.

Administrative stuff

The absolute minimum, sufficient to identify the author and the project to which the report applies.

Author's project responsibilities

A summary section of where the experience report author fitted into the scheme of things—the responsibilities from which the stated experience flowed.

An important part of this section is that of responsibilities that the author had towards other groups/team members; also of the responsibilities that they had towards the author. It is often in the area of intergroup working—probably *the* characteristic which differentiates projects which need a formal software engineering approach from those that do not—that the biggest problems arise. Authors should know that their experiences in working with other groups are part and parcel of what is expected from their reports.

Lessons learned

A simple checklist could be useful here, although it is much more important to allow writers to get across the major points of their experience than to feel they have to work laboriously through a long list of possibly irrelevant topics.

Perhaps gentle guidance is no more than is necessary:

- Did you achieve what you set out to do?
- What worked well?
- What could have been done better?
- Was anything omitted?
- What have you learnt from working on the project?

If the development process has measures, some of these lessons will be identifiable simply by looking at which measures were met, which missed and which exceeded.

Recommendations

The key part of any experience report. Knowing what went wrong is helpful, but knowing how to avoid the problem next time is worth much more.

Recommendations should, wherever possible, be related to changes in process, in other words, how do we do better next time? Process is the permanent factor, not project-specific details. It is also a useful antidote to emotion. For instance, it might be a developer's recommendation that, 'never again should we develop software in the SPLODGE language'. This may be the developer's heartfelt view, but it is a view of the heart. Concentrating on the process, however, would produce a rather more constructive, 'an improved process for selecting an implementation language is needed; language SPLODGE was wholly unsuitable'.

It should be clearly understood that report authors are expected not only to identify their lessons learned but also to make recommendations. This has the doubly beneficial effects of making authors feel that what they are doing is worth while, and of removing the idle, nonconstructive 'whinge items' from the reports.

There should be very few constraints, if any, about the sort of recommendations that can be made. What you are looking for is a degree of imagination—especially as many of the experiences are likely to be examples of *déjà vu*.

The only stipulation worth making about a recommendation is that it comes accompanied by a subrecommendation as to how any future action should be tracked, by whom, and by when. Nothing devalues a lessons-learned process more quickly than having agreed actions not carried out—and no action is simpler to agree to than that which cannot be tracked to completion.

12.2.2   Timing

The only area in which it is important to be firm is in that of timing. Procrastination cannot be tolerated. Arguments about experience capture not being worth the effort because people are moving on to other things will be self-fulfilling if too much time is allowed for the exercise.

Require that experience reports be produced within a very short period of time (say two weeks) of project completion. This will not only guarantee that the exercise is completed but also be an incentive to do it. With a culture in which defect prevention processes are a way of life, long-running projects should present no problem.

As part of the planning activity, experience capture checkpoints would be determined—normally to coincide with the end of some development/test activity. The procedure is as outlined above. Reports can then be amalgamated into a single report when the project is finally complete or left as a set of individual reports. In this way the inevitable changes of personnel do not result in a loss of experience; moreover, neither do changes of plan. In fact it may well be that a significant plan change could be used as a trigger for an experience capture exercise.

12.3   A postship review process

Producing a postship experience report is a way of capturing the individual's view of how things went; the risks encountered, and how they were resolved. Opinions will differ, of course. Christopher Columbus' views on his voyage around the world almost certainly differed from the views of the ship's cook (who probably complained about his lack of a decent view for a start). Both are important, though. The lessons that would have been passed on to future round-the-world travellers would have dealt not only with navigation risks and how they were managed, but also with other risks such as the crew contracting scurvy through the lack of a well-balanced diet.

That is why the various lessons have to consolidated into what we might call the 'team experience'—a coherent set of lessons applicable at the macro- rather than the micro-level. This consolidation activity is the function of the postship review process.

12.3.1   Objectives

The process should be geared towards examining the performance of the whole production team. This is not to say that individual lessons will be lost: far from it. They will have already been captured through the experience report and they must not be lost. What the review process seeks to do, however, is to see if it possible to build on them and discover lessons that need to be learned at the team level.

That said, the primary focus areas of the review are likely to be:

- The development organization and its structure
- The development process
- The change control processes
- Project management and associated tools
- Development tools in general
- Administrative support (such as information systems support, finance, and administrative services)

12.3.2   Ownership of the process

A tricky one. The obvious choice is for the product manager to own the postship review process. This is sensible, but it is important, perhaps with this process more than any other, to emphasize the distinction between the ownership of a process and the conduct of that process.

The owner is not necessarily the best person to conduct a postship review. In fact, we might go so far as to state the opposite: if the product manager owns the postship review process for the product then that person is definitely not the best to conduct a postship review.

Why? Consider Christopher Columbus again. Would the cook speak as freely about the ship's deplorable lack of cooking utensils, and about how he was forced to improvise with all manner of weird and unhygenic items, if the captain himself was conducting the review? Possibly.

Conversely, would the captain be inclined to dig deeper into the problem if he suspected the answer would lay the blame at his own cabin door? Again, possibly. But only if he had considered it to be a problem in the first place, which, because of his own perspective (food did keep appearing in front of him, after all), might not be the case. Furthermore, remember we are looking for the team view to pass on to other teams. The captain is close—almost certainly too close—to what has happened to be sufficiently objective about it.

Ownership of the process by the product manager is important then, because the product manager's support is necessary to ensure that the review is taken seriously. *Conduct* of the review, however, is best undertaken by somebody—or some team of bodies—a little more detached. An assurance team is perfect for the task. An acceptable alternative would be a cross-product team led by a senior member of another development group—ideally a group that had a vested interest in learning from the experiences of the team under review. Whoever conducts it, some ground rules have to be established. The most important is that there are no recriminations: the review is being held to learn how to do things better in the future, for everybody's benefit.

12.3.3 Process steps

The steps in the process are as follows.

Establish review team

The review team, a team which could be as small as two people, needs to be set up. The establishment of this team is the one task that should be carried out by the product manager, who has the 'clout' necessary to get the right people on the team.

Who are the right people? Ideally, peer professionals and managers from other product areas. They should have sufficient experience to be aware of the key areas to examine and the questions most needing to be asked, and should also command enough respect within the organization to get answers to those questions when they ask them. Consider including customer representatives, so that customer feedback can be taken into account.

Advance warning!

Once the review team is established, the team leader should inform everybody who was involved with the project in any way that a review is to be held. The review team leader should stress to members that *now* is the time for experience reports to be written if they have not already been done.

Experience gathering

There are various ways in which this part of the exercise can be carried out by the review team:

1   They can collect experience reports and sift through them to produce a list of lessons learned and recommendations. This is heavy on review team time, but has the useful by-product of focusing attention on the need to produce an experience report by a certain date.
2   They can hold a review meeting. This is an efficient method, especially if the number of people involved in the project was relatively small. At the meeting, all contributors make short presentations of the key lessons from their experience reports (a maximum of three good points and three bad points, say). Such a meeting not only enables the exercise to be conducted relatively quickly, but also gives the review team the opportunity to clarify points which might otherwise take a little flurry of email to resolve.
3   A more time-consuming way is for members of the review team to interview contributors on a one-to-one basis. This is obviously much harder work. It may, however, be the best approach to reviewing a project that was very complex, that fared rather badly and/or that had larger-than-usual levels of friction associated with it.

The initial review summary

At this stage the review team produce a draft consolidated summary of all lessons and associated recommendations they have received. The 'all' is important. If the exercise is to be seen as valuable and worthy of spending time and effort on, then at the very least all participants should see their contributions—in some shape or form—end up in the review summary document.

Inevitably, some form of editing will take place. Similar comments will be combined, lengthy diatribes may be condensed, and so on. For this reason it is a good idea for the draft summary to be sent out to all participants so that they can confirm or deny that they really did say what the document has quoted them as saying.

This initial review summary must not delay matters, however. The review team's concern is to complete the exercise, and they should set a 'by return of post' deadline for any comments back.

Action items and owners

The review team take on their most important task. With the lessons learned and recommendations (plus any comments received) before them, they then set out to identify action items and, more importantly, action owners for each point made.

Action items flow naturally from recommendations that the review participants have made, and will often amount to exactly the same set of words. What the team should do, however, is to spot instances in which the recommendations have a wider applicability than simply that of the product area under review. This is particularly the case where development processes are concerned. Thus reworking product-specific recommendations into recommendations in a more generic form is an important part of the team's remit. Action owners need to be identified, and this is where the value of having an experienced, cross-product review team is seen. They should be in a position to know who in their organization is best placed to make things happen. This is not to say, of course, that the nominated owners will agree with the review team on this matter! That is where the next stage of the review process fits in.

Obtain commitments

The bulk of the review document should now resemble Table 12.1. This interim review summary is now circulated to the identified action owners with a fairly simple question list:

1   Do you agree that you own the recommendations and actions that this document has allocated to you?
2   If you do, what action do you propose to take?
3   If you do not,
    (a)   Explain why not (e.g., the costs are too high), and
    (b)   Suggest the name of a more suitable owner.

The method employed is simplicity itself, especially if the interim document can be circulated as softcopy: the nominated action owners simply complete the fourth column and return the document to the review team. The objective of this part of the exercise is not, as the above list should suggest, to present the review recommendations as a *fait accompli*. It is perfectly possible for a nominated owner to say 'no, thank you' or to accept ownership of the problem but to suggest that the most appropriate action is no action at all. Here, again, is an important function of the review team and another reason why they should be well-respected; the team must analyse the action owner's responses and, if any are considered inadequate, go back and argue.

The final postship review summary

Ultimately, all will be decided. Action owners will have accepted their responsibilities and devised plans to meet them. In completing the remaining part of the

Table 12.1.   Postship review—lessons learned and recommendations

Number	Comment	Recommendation	Owner	Response/action
1	Programmer did not know language SPLODGE when work started	An internal training course on SPLODGE should be set up. The course shown be given to all new programmers.	Training manager	
2	Suspicion that initial code sizings too low	Set up task force to review techniques for code sizing to see whether improvement is needed.	Technical planning	
3	Some parts of module XYZ are not as efficient as they could be	Before we start on release 2 we should carry out an optimization scan to see what can be improved.	Mgr product X release 2	

interim document the final report has virtually been produced. The bulk of it will look much as Table 12.2. A minimal amount of t-crossing and i-dotting will be all that is needed to finish it off.

Tracking

In the perfect world, that would be the end of it. All action owners would honour their commitments, processes would be improved, etc., and all future projects would benefit through not making the same mistakes as their predecessors. Unfortunately, the world is far from perfect. Tracking actions is the necessary final step in the process. The review team should ensure that agreements are reached about how the identified actions are to be tracked, and by whom. Ideally, the product managers or their representative should carry the ultimate responsibility for this.

Only when all actions have been carried out, should the postship review be considered complete.

12.3.4 *How long will it take?*

All of the above might sound like a never-ending exercise. And so it could be, if allowed. The review team should ensure that this is not the case. Procrastination is the kiss of death to a postship review. The whole process must be driven along

Table 12.2.   Postship review—actions

Number	Comment	Recommendation	Owner	Response/action
1	Programmer did not know language SPLODGE when work started	An internal training course on SPLODGE should be set up. The course should be given to all new programmers.	Training manager	A SPLODGE multi-media self-study course has been ordered. It will be available for use within two months; a review will be conducted after the package has been in use for six months.
2	Suspicion that initial code sizings too low	Set up task force to review techniques for code sizing to see whether improvement is needed.	Technical planning	I already have a small team looking at the available tools for code sizing. The team will promulgate their findings through the software tools council. This, I believe is sufficient action for now.
3	Some parts of module XYZ not as efficient as they could be	Before we start release 2 we should carry out an optimization scan to see what can be improved.	Mgr product X release 2	Requirement for optimization scan added to requirements database for release 2. Priority to be allocated at requirements review scheduled for xx/xx/xx.

briskly: not so fast that contributors have no time to think about their inputs, but neither so slow that they have time to forget and/or flee the country.

Obviously, the duration of the exercise will depend on the size of the project being reviewed and the approaches taken to gather the information. At one extreme, for a 100+ person-year project, with review interviews being conducted, expect the whole process to take at least 4 weeks; for a small project of a few person-years, less than a week should be sufficient.

12.4   Now I hope you have learned your lesson!

A successful postship review, then, is a generator of actions to ensure that good experiences are repeated and that bad experiences are not. Where those actions can be translated into process changes, the lessons are 'learned' by future projects automatically—assuming they follow the process, that is.

How will we know? The only real way, as we have been saying whenever processes have been mentioned in this book, is to define and use a measure. How can 'lessons learned' be measured? 'With great difficulty' is the only possible answer. We are talking about something ephemeral here. Are we trying to count lessons which are learned once, or for ever? Is our yardstick of success to be that of not seeing the same risk next time round, or of never, ever, seeing it again? Do we apply the condition to future releases of the product just reviewed, or to every release of every product that our organization produces between now and eternity?

The answer is probably 'all—but one would be a good start'. For we cannot avoid the fact that people are the key element in learning lessons; some may be learned at once, others may have to be learned time and time again. Was it ever thus—we are human, after all.

There is perhaps more progress to be made in looking at the question from a different angle. Lessons are very often not learned simply because they have not been recorded. To put it another way: ensuring that good experience reports are produced and postship reviews are held is half the battle. So, can we gain by focusing measurement on the extent to which the experience-capturing process has worked?

12.4.1 A 'lessons learned' measure

Various binary measures suggest themselves:

- Experience reports are/are not produced.
- A postship review is/is not conducted.
- Findings of the postship review are/are not accepted by the nominated action owners.
- Actions are/are not carried out as promised.

More imaginative measures might be based on the following.

Timeliness

Are the various process steps achieved within a 'target' time? Dawdling is the biggest danger to capturing experience. With every day that passes beyond the completion of a project, better and better excuses can be constructed for not taking part in a lessons-learned process. Tracking elapsed days beyond what is reasonable is a simple but effective way of preventing drift by default.

Quality

Horribly subjective, of course, but by measuring in some way the 'quality' of experience reports and post-ship reviews it may be possible to gauge how well the exercise has been carried out. A not unreasonable projection is that good experience-capturing will be matched by correspondingly good attention to the lessons learned.

So, why not measure such aspects as:

- Accuracy—how many points were disputed?
- Completeness—how many omissions were identified?
- Customer 'satisfaction'—did all concerned accept what was said, even though they may not have liked it?

Implementation

Ideally, we are are looking for corrective actions to be put into place. It is a bit like entering a competition. Put your entry form in and there is a chance you may win. Do not put it in and there is no chance. So, although implementing an action is no guarantee that its associated risk, like Dracula, will not rise again, at least it lessens the chances.

There is value in measuring, therefore:

- The proportion of identified 'lessons learned' that were accepted as valid
- The proportion of recommendations that were accepted and implemented.

There are no 'right' answers here. Imaginative accounting is called for, so long as the bottom line offers an answer to the question: 'Have we learnt our lesson?'

13
And round to the beginning again

We are all good risk managers. A project manager coming to the end of a project will be an even better one. You will be more 'experienced'. Experience for most project managers is a euphemism for the sort of grisly mental torture that leaves them mentally scarred for life; but it need not be so. As we have seen in the previous chapters, there is a strategy for dealing with circumstances before they become pathological.

By 'experience' (the right kind, that is), we really mean three things:

- Models—some intelligent expectation of the way things work
- Data—hard facts and figures from the way things worked in the last project
- Confidence—belief in the models and data, and the willingness to apply them in the future

Armed with this kind of experience, you are better equipped to tackle the next project. Each of these three factors is now discussed in more detail.

13.1   Models

A recurring theme throughout this book, first introduced in Chapter 4, is the use of a process. Using a process allows a methodical and repeatable way of working, within which one can make sense of the way that things behave, in both a quantitative and a qualitative sense. Key to the quantitative sense, of course, is the collection of data, discussed below, and this is vital for turning into simple models, such as productivity rates, proportionality between stages, defect rates, etc. But there is the deeper intuitive understanding of the software project world that comes from a sense of order and discipline that is imposed on it.

The software project is a world of its own. There are different cultures, such as programmers, analysts, testers, users, and maybe planners, marketeers, writers, editors, and so on. Each of these cultures will have its own customs, its own agendas, and its own way of thinking. Making sense out of this ethnic diversity and drawing all together into one community with a common purpose is not going to succeed if it depends solely upon your diplomatic skills. You are not going to be able to foist the IT equivalent of the Euro-sausage on the whole project.

If each group has its own process *which is visible, and known to all the others*, then the problems will not all go away, but there will be a much better basis for exercising those diplomatic skills, because your understanding of the logical relationships between, and needs of, the different groups will complement their mutual understandings.

This intuitive appreciation of working relationships both within and between these different cultures is the basis for your internal project modelling that will be of enormous value in succeeding projects. Remember, a model is simply an expectation of what will happen, and models are much more readily built within a process framework.

13.2   Data

In a perfect world, you would have a project database filled with complete and well-organized data relating to all phases of the project that was analysed and ready for transfer into your next project. Realistically, the data you have collected is probably disorganized, incomplete, and dispersed over a number of different cabinet drawers and computer files. The significant thing is that the data exists; it would be criminal not to use it. Make a note of what data you have. At the very least, collate it, and make sure it is available for future use. If you can afford the luxury of applying someone to the task of analysing the data, have them calculate, in whatever units are appropriate, all the productivity rates and defect rates from the different phases, and the proportions of effort spent on the different phases.

For next time round, what you need are numbers. That means some useful information derived from the mass of data, like the ones suggested above: information that you can use for planning, as rules of thumb for reasonableness checks, and for comparing against other people's claims. You either need those numbers immediately to hand, or know where you can derive them quickly. You will know all about your own data; it helps to know what other people have stored away. Find out what data has been collected by other projects.

We have referred to the need for some sort of integrated project data storage. Having been through the cycle once and seen the need to refer back to the data that you have collected, now is the time to install that system that will make life so much easier in the future.

13.3   Confidence

There is not a lot to say about this one. All who have arrived at a more-or-less successful conclusion to a difficult project by the application of their intellectual horsepower to the identification and management of risk now will not only be willing but more able to repeat the exercise. They will have a better appreciation of their own technical strengths: whether it is in the analytical and logical approach to planning and tracking, or in the flashes of creative genius that characterize their solutions to problems.

Whatever your own approach, thinking the thing through, testing the validity of your thinking, and working out where and why your assumptions were wrong teaches a lot about software risk management in a comparatively short time. Confidence comes from not only being willing and able, but also knowing that you will be able to do it even better next time.

13.4   Passing it on

In the medieval guilds, knowledge of the trade (trade secrets) was jealously guarded by the masters. Apprentices had to pay for that knowledge, both financially and through long and tedious time spent on trivial tasks.

It would be facile to suggest that things are not much better now, but there is no easy way for a project manager to learn the trade on the job. There are formal courses, but that is theoretical knowledge that has to be applied later without support from the course leader.

Consider taking on an apprentice. You will then have someone who can learn from your experience, and see it applied in practical situations. You will have someone who, in the manner of apprentices in the past, can help with those tasks that are so difficult to get started on, such as data analysis. You will also have someone who can take over from you if necessary, and you will have the satisfaction of knowing that you have done your bit towards improving the professionalism of your IT world.

This can work both ways. If you feel somewhat out of your depth in the project that you have responsibility for, consider asking for a mentor from among the more experienced managers of your acquaintance. Alternatively, try and make a reciprocal arrangement with another manager to review each other's project at appropriate intervals (peer review). This means that you both gain from the experience of looking at a broader range of projects than you would otherwise see.

13.5   And the next project

The postmortem is over, the customer has the product, most of your project staff have gone to their next projects, and you have your next assignment. You are full of confidence, your new customers are full of expectations, and you have a clean sheet of paper in front of you.

What is different this time? Well, the target language is different, so there will have to be training, provision made for a learning curve, the productivity rate will probably be different, so where will I get some information on that? Did Jack run a project using C? And how am I going to prototype the user interface? . . .

We are all good risk managers . . . .

Appendix 1
Process template

The following checklist contains potential items for your written process. Not all of the items may be applicable to your process, but be sure to read and think about each before you decide to exclude it.

The order of sections is as recommended for the final process, but in writing the process, you should complete 'user' first, followed by 'customer' and 'objective'. Remember that you are writing the process for users, so that they can fulfil an objective, and satisfy their customers.

You may like to begin with some general background or context material.

Objective

What is the process to achieve? If this process is used once, what can an individual expect to achieve (e.g., this process allows you to run a successful group meeting). The process must always be relatable to the mission and strategy of the department, group and company, and must have been validated by its customers.

Scope

The potential user needs to be able to work out whether or not this process is relevant. Say what the scope of the process is. For example, if the process will only work in a mainframe environment, or when there is an 'r' in the month, say so.

Owner

Who is responsible for keeping the process current (continual improvement)? You may also wish to list your team members, but make clear which of you carries the ultimate responsibility.

Customers

Who are the recipients of the output (work product) of the process?

User

Who will use the process? What sort of skill level is required? Write the rest of the process with this person in mind.

Entry

What does the user need to start, and who will supply it? Be absolutely precise. For example, if you need an approved plan, say 'approved plan', not 'plan'.

Activity

What does the user do? Itemize step by step. The final step should always be: 'Self-examine use of process, and feed back measures and suggestions for improvement to the process owner', or some formal defect prevention activity, until this becomes second nature in your organization's culture.

Input

What does the user need from others during use of the process, from whom and when? Think how this relates to your (or your department's) critical success factors; the critical needs you have on others to fulfil your own mission.

Supplier

The person or group who supplies your input.

Output

What must be supplied to others during the process, to whom and when? (See also 'tracking'.)

Exit

What does the user end up with? What does the user hand to the customers?

Verification

How will the user of the process verify that the output is an accurate translation of the input in the approved format?

Validation

How will the user of the process validate that the output matches customer requirements, or better still, delights the customer?

Change process

What is the equivalent change process to this process? For example, for the high-level design process, where is there a process to a similar level of detail and control for changing the design produced by this process?

Timing

When is the process run?

Data

Identify any data which this process needs to permit world-class decision-making and management (and suggests which process supplies this data).

Schedule

How long will it take? What resource is required? It is likely that you will wish to point to experience data elsewhere, or better still, to a tool or automated planning system, but please ensure it exists first, or produce a plan to set it up.

Tracking

What intermediate data should be supplied as this process is run, to enable the user to tell if it is running according to plan? Explain precisely what the data is, what information it will supply to further proper control (see below), how it will be extracted, normalized and presented, and the kind of control it will therefore permit.

Control

If the process is found not to be running to plan, what kinds of control can be exercised so that the required output is still delivered completely, within budget and on time? Think of ways of tracking progress and ways of getting back on target if behind.

Business controls

On the continued operation of this process.

Tools

What might help the user complete the process faster/better/at all?

Responsibilities

Who does which bits? The best processes are run by one person. If the steps in your process seem to be run by many different people, think about splitting it up.

Sign-off

Who is responsible for affirming that the process is complete and ready for exit? Is it entirely delegated to the process user, or is it merely referred, requiring management sign-off?

Education

Are there any courses to help the user acquire the right skills to use the process, or educational or background reading material? If your company has 'hot buttons', put them here.

References

Where might the user get more help, while performing the job?

Conventions

Are there any hidden musts (usually from requirements not reflected in the main objective, such as internal politics, or whatever)?

Measurement

The process has an objective. Say what measures should be made by the user to demonstrate that it was achieved on time, and explain where you (the process owner) will be collating the results.

Metrics

Are there any other metrics which could be made in this process and would be useful elsewhere, for example the next time round? If your process collects data, be sure you understand how it will be used by others to fulfil one of their objectives. Remember that there is no point in collecting data which no one plans to use.

Causal analysis

How/when will you handle defects in this process?

Process changes

How will you manage changes to this process?

Value

List the benefits of using this process and quantify the savings of each use in financial terms.

Judgement

If the use of the process requires no judgement, it can probably be automated. If you can describe the sorts of judgement required by this process, it will help ensure that processes are run by people with the right skills.

Risk

List the risks attached to using the process.

Costs

Quantify the cost of running the process.

History

Experience with/comment on this process/dates of current version and next revision.

Appendix 2
Documenting the risk management strategy and plan

A2.1 Objective

Prepare a plan for managing risk which:

- Defines the scope of the risk assessment work
- Identifies the high and medium risk areas of the project
- Defines specific risk management tasks for these areas
- Explains which of the standard processes will be used for low-risk monitoring
- Is written in consultation with the development team
- Is agreed with appropriate levels of management, and can become a common understanding of the work to be done
- Explains how executing the plan will be tracked and its success measured
- Is better than previous plans

A2.2 Customers

Bear in mind that your plan has customers. (Why else would you write it?) These customers are:

- The project manager (if not the risk assessor)
- You and your team (so you can perform the work in a planned way)
- You and your manager, if different from the project manager (so you can track your work)
- Future assessors (by planning time to improve processes based on your experience)
- The auditor (did we use our processes?)

You will be expecting the development team to be writing good plans later. If you can do your own plan well, it will serve as a good example.

A2.3   Input

Familiarize yourself with the following, if they are available:

- The project's process.
- The project's schedule.
- The project's requirements, objectives and specifications.
- The project's comprehensive project plan and associated plans. It is probable that the comprehensive product plan will be evolving as you write your RMP. You will need to keep in touch with its development. 'Comprehensive project plan' is a plan which details what all development areas will be doing between now and the next checkpoint.
- The development team (the individuals rather than the organization chart).

If some of these are not available, at least as far as the next checkpoint, you may have found your first risk areas.

A2.4   Activity

1   Agree a production schedule for the work.
2   You may like to produce a risk management strategy before the plan so you do not go off too far at a tangent. A template is given in Appendix 3.
3   If you are working on a joint project with another location, you can ensure that the scope of your risk work is clearly bounded by an agreed document of understanding (DOU) before proceeding. It will also be useful to identify the deliverables which will pass between you and your counterparts during the project. A sample DOU template is given in Appendix 7.
4   Identify areas of high or medium risk within the project during this development phase. You may find the techniques we suggested earlier useful for this.
5   For each of the areas you have identified as being high or medium risk make a clear and concise statement of what the risk is.
6   For high risk areas, plan activities to influence product management into reducing the risk:

   (a)   Use history and experience as much as possible. For a multirelease project analyse the approach adopted last time and try to improve on it. Recall the problems; consider how they might have been avoided. Look at experience reports from previous related projects.

   (b)   Consider the benefits of prototyping, modelling, simulation, etc., as ways of reducing risk.

   (c)   Assess the need for independent peer reviews, joint involvement in tests and experiments, and loan of risk management skills to development. Any commitment to supply resource to development must be clearly and concisely documented, so both sides are aware of the precise nature of the commitments.

Try to give every activity an objective and a measure.

7   For medium risk areas, plan activities to contain the risk.

8   For low risk areas, nominate the processes you will use to monitor these areas. Do not duplicate the process descriptions in your plan. Further information on monitoring expectations appear in the MORE section of this book, but the general rule should be:

(a)   What is the risk you are trying to spot?

(b)   What should you look at on a regular basis to know if the risk is materializing?

(c)   What is the best (simplest or clearest) way of presenting this information? (Think of the various chart types you could use: histograms, line graphs, timelines, GANTT charts, etc.)

9   Now devise plans to eliminate, control, or monitor the risks, remembering to calculate the effort you would have to put into this risk management compared with the cost you may be saving.

10   Document your RMP. A template for this appears in Appendix 4.

11   Have the plan reviewed by team leaders in your group, and one or two risk assessment peers from other projects. It is probably best to invite them to a meeting to review the plan. The need for this step will probably depend on the level of experience of the author. Hold the meeting, and update the plan.

12   Review and agree the plan with your manager. If the assessment peers do not agree, and you have conceded as much as you believe to be in the best interest of your company and your customer, they should be prepared to escalate you (i.e. take their concerns to your next level of management) within a reasonable time frame.

13   Educate the rest of the team of the content of your final plan. If you have spotted risks, it is best to tell everyone so they can all take part in the neighbourhood risk watch.

14   Review the plan with other locations if appropriate.

15   Keep your plan accessible and up to date.

A2.5   Output

Approved RMP.

A2.6   Timing

You should complete the above process by one month after IBP exit, or within one month of starting work, whichever is later.

A2.7   Measurement

There is a binary measurement on the production of the plan. The plan either exists or it does not. It is either in the approved form or not. But how much effort has been put into determining the contents, and how effective will it be?

1   At one level, you could measure that the project completes on time with all the originally agreed requirements (function, usability, etc.). But ultimately this is the responsibility of the product manager, and there may be other influences which could cause the project to fail. So at best this is an indicator rather than a measure of success.
2   At a second level you could try and measure achievement of your mission: that you kept management informed of all the risks in a timely fashion; that you made management understand all the risks, even though they may have judged these risks against other factors and taken a decision to proceed.
3   At a third level, you could measure that you met all the planned objectives (influenced all the identified high risks, contained all the medium risks, and were not surprised by any unexpected risks materializing)

A2.8   References

- RMPs for other similar projects (to gain more ideas about risks and topical techniques for avoiding them)
- RMPs for other recent projects
- List of risks which happened on recent projects

Appendix 3
Risk management strategy template

A3.1 Information sources

List where you found inspiration for this strategy—defect databases are a good source, especially if they describe the really big risks that materialized on other recent products. Experience reports for previous projects and RMPs for other current projects can be useful, and a brainstorm among the team members can suggest where the experts think the risks are.

A3.2 General risk directions

Talk about the current hot buttons in risk management, the state-of-the-art risks and risk management techniques.

A3.3 Risk minimization techniques

Describe the techniques you plan to use, for example, some words about ensuring adherence to processes, process tailoring and customer focus would not go amiss, along with any other ideas for avoiding risks.

A3.4 Risk assessment strategy

Talk in general terms about how you plan to get information to assess and evaluate risks, prioritize them and appraise management of risks and solutions.

A3.5 Specific project risks

It may be that you can already see some specific risk areas for this project. If so, list them.

A3.6 Resources

Say something about the risk assessment staffing emphasis (early investment versus late firefighting), ways in which the risk assessor will liaise with the team, and so on.

A3.7 Plan schedule

Details of when detailed risk assessment plans will be available in draft and approved form (and who will produce them). It is recommended that a plan is agreed prior to exit from each checkpoint, which will last till the next checkpoint.

Appendix 4
Template for a risk management plan

This is a risk management plan template for you to copy and modify to reflect your plan for managing risk on your project. The earlier sections of this book tell you of the context in which you might write such a plan, and other activities which go with it. The instructions in this template are just to do with writing down the results of those activities.

Remember who your audience is, as you write the plan out. If you are the project manager, it is probably your manager. If you are an independent risk assessor, it is probably the project manager. Whichever, this plan can act as a contract, or scope of work.

You would do well to start with a BS5750-compliant cover page. We leave you to find out how to do that. But think about the currency of your plan. How far into the future are you planning today? Is it for the whole project life, or just to the next checkpoint? We would recommend using checkpoints and updating the plan at each. Whatever you decide, write the following control information accordingly.

A4.1   Preliminary pages

A4.1.1 Objective

The plan should define its own objective, currency and function. For example: 'This plan describes the planned risk assessment activity for Project X from Initial Business Proposal through to Commit Checkpoint.'

A4.1.2 Reviewers

List all the people who have reviewed the plan during production. The more information you can give, the easier it will be for your approver to approve the plan.

180

A4.1.3 Issues and concerns

Issues and concerns are unfinished business—perhaps there are items in your plan with which your approvers and reviewers do not agree. If there are any issues or concerns with the content of this plan, list them here. It will make it easier when you go 'around again'.

A4.1.4 Distribution list

List all the people who will have a copy of the plan. Some projects may well operate a project database, where the plan can be stored, alongside other project plans, eliminating the need for a large distribution.

A4.1.5 References

Do not duplicate information in your RMP which can be found elsewhere. Instead, make a list here of other sources of information, and where they can be obtained. Remember to date any references you have used which may be updated later.

The body of the document starts here. It consists of a set of headings, comments and boxes to fill in.

A4.2   Introduction

It is useful to have a single-page summary of a project which can be used to form a section in monthly reports and can go in the risk plan, the experience report, or to send to a new contact. It has three sections, and you can avoid excessive detail by pointing at project documents referenced earlier. Tailor the list according to what you feel is important.

A4.2.1 Brief project description

Brief description—what the project fundamentally is in a few sentences.

A4.2.2 Project facts

Project manager	Howard y'Do
Project number	IAM1
Program number	5664–196
Product type	Program product
Vendor	Blue-of-the-night
Development code	2KCSI, 67 KSSI in assembler H

Development resource	35 programmers
Service category	Class B
Operating environment	OS/2
Strategic prereqs	EWAS1.2
Prereq. product for	IAM3
Major competitors	None

A4.2.3 Key dates

- Project start
- Initial business approval
- Vendor contract signed
- Announcement (commercial products)
- General availability of product
- End of service

Tell your readers you will not be updating your plan every time project dates change, and where up-to-date dates can be found. The following sentences could be amplified:

> Disclaimer: the reader should note that the dates in this section are only current on the day the plan is approved. Project sources should be contacted for up-to-date information.

A4.3   Risk assessment overview

A4.3.1 Risk model analysis

Chapter 4 explained some general techniques for assessing risk. Hopefully you have done some of this and have some idea of how this project compares with others in terms of the overall risk. This will have given you some rough ideas about the staffing levels required for risk work and may have given some early indication of risk areas. Put a copy of the output from this high-level analysis here. Table A4.1 is a sample format for the section. Use this or invent your own, but be sure to say who ran the model (assessor and developer) and when. Experience with

Table A4.1.   Sample format

Element	Value	Score	Weight	Total
Total				

Run by.............................   date.....................

recent products also suggests that it will be worth rerunning the global risk model at each product checkpoint.

You may also like to say what conclusions the risk model has allowed you to draw about the kind of assessments to plan.

A4.3.2 Improvements

List ways in which the method you are planning to manage risk on this project is better than any you or your department have ever done before. If there are none, say so. Possible plus points include:

- Using this enhanced process for writing your plan
- Using new techniques as a result of recommendations from past experience reports
- Improving the efficiency of your assessment

If possible, quantify the improvements.

A4.3.3 Lessons learned

You may like to:
- Identify a predecessor or best-of-breed product
- Describe what lessons you have learned from it
- Justify any experience from that project which you will not be using on this

If you update your processes, focus areas, and so on, as experience reports are produced, it may be adequate to say that lessons are learned in that way.

A4.3.4 Division of work

If this is split location (or department) risk assessment work, summarize the DOU (see Appendix 7) with your counterparts here in a few sentences, and point at it.

A4.3.5 Location of work

If there are any geographical peculiarities about the risk work describe them here. Planned trips, assignments and so on could be usefully summarized.

A4.3.6 Deviations

For audit reasons, you should indicate which aspects of the RMP process you omitted or changed. Ignoring the process is your risk, but be aware you are taking it. List how you have deviated from the process in producing this plan. For each deviation give a single sentence justification.

A4.4   Strategy

If there is an overall risk management strategy for this product, you might describe it here. This is not the general strategy, but any specific notes pertaining to your department, or the product family and the way this product fits in. Appendix 2 told you how to do this.

There should be a risk management strategy for every project within a month of starting the project.

A4.4.1 Assessment of risk areas

The essential ingredients are:

- Perform a risk assessment on the project.
- Say here what technique you used. If it is one from a standard process set, just name it.
- Say how often risks will be re-evaluated.
- List the high risks.
- For each high risk describe your plan to change the product plan.
- List the medium risks.
- For each medium risk, describe your plan to get development to contain it.

You may also wish to list the low risks you will monitor during the project. Be conscious as you do this of how much effort will be expended on the risk activity and compare it with the corresponding expected saving to the project.

A4.4.2 Issue tracking

If you highlight a risk and the person you identify to address it refuses to listen to you, you have an issue. A common problem is that having highlighted a risk, it is waved in the air and forgotten about. Describe the process by which you will log and track issues, to ensure that everything you identify is followed through to satisfactory completion at the right level of management.

A4.4.3 Value add

Risk assessment is what you are supposed to be doing. But if you can offer any added value to the project, please describe it here. Suggestions could include:

- Investment items
- Helping the project team try out new techniques
- Consultancy (from our centres of competence)

A4.4.4 Assessment DOUs with other locations

Are you working with other locations? If so, you should have a DOU with each. Say how you plan to achieve this, with whom and/or when.

A4.5   Risk assessment deliverables

The aim of this section is to make specific plans for real people to deliver them at promised times. If you want to begin this section with a general communication strategy do. The following specific subject headings should be considered.

A4.5.1 Risk assessments

What risk assessment reports will you produce during the course of the project, with what content, by whom, to whom and at what frequency? Here you should describe plans to report your prognoses to development managers, at development tracking meetings and to other locations.

A useful format for doing this is shown in Table A4.2. In evaluating the duration in the final column, do not forget time to prepare and time to tidy up loose ends afterwards.

Table A4.2.   Sample format for risk assessment reports

Task	Who	Frequency	Time	Hrs
Monthly report to executive management	ABC	Monthly	First week	18
Product manager contact meeting	DEF	Monthly	Last week	
Attend project status meeting	DEF	Weekly	Thurs a.m.	
⋮	⋮	⋮	⋮	⋮

A4.5.2 Key date assessments

When you produce your monthly report, you will regularly forecast against certain key items (e.g., announce, availability, system test start). List here which key items you plan to forecast.

A4.5.3 Checkpoint/phase position/key date plan

You may wish to take stop/go positions at checkpoints. If this plan is to be at all meaningful, you should be able to plan all the positions to take during its currency. A sample format is shown in Table A4.3.

A4.5.4 Other deliverables

This is an optional section for anything you have not mentioned yet but want to.

Table A4.3. Sample format for checkpoints plan

Checkpoint	Plan	Actual	Who	Process

Initial business proposal
  Start position preparation
  Package complete
  Technical review
  Business review
  Exit				

Commitment
  Start position preparation
  Technical review
  Business review
  Exit				

Shipment
  Start position preparation
  Technical review
  Business review
  Exit
  GA				

A4.5.5 Tracking the progress of the risk management activities

For management tracking purposes, it may be useful to list your proposed activities on a tracking chart (Table A4.4) which can be presented at a regular tracking meetings. Describe when these meetings will occur, also, when wider reviews will be undertaken. If this RMP contains any unresolved dates (e.g., test entry/exit) list the dates by which you plan to resolve them. If this plan will not run for the entire project, give the dates for producing the next revision. Finally, give planned dates for the experience report (or reports if you are producing them by phase).

Table A4.4. Activity tracking chart

Planned item	Plan	Actual
⋮		
Re-evaluate overall project risk for next checkpoint RMP—next draft RMP approval Experience report draft Experience report approved		

A4.6   Resources and dependencies

What assumptions have been made in this plan which are not yet fulfilled? For example, do you need any more hardware, software, people, tools or education to do the job? Are there any other entry criteria (things you need before particular activities can be started)? These items should be defined by risk area and then gathered here.

A4.6.1 Resource allocation and schedule details

The risk analysis should have led you to identify particular assessment tasks which you can allocate to individuals and schedule here. Table A4.5 may be a useful format. It can also be used as a tracking table.

Table A4.5.   Sample format for resource and schedule allocation

Task	Who	Start	End	Hrs
⋮				

A4.6.2 Resource estimates

Estimate the total manpower required by month to complete your work according to this plan. For some projects, it may be that the manpower is allocated prior to the identification of risks! The planning exercise would then involve prioritizing the risks, estimating how long each would take to influence, and ignoring all risks below the threshhold of available manpower.

Whichever technique is used, the resourcing must be agreed with your management, and it is always advisable to allocate some slack to cover risks which cannot be identified when the plan is drawn up: 25 per cent is recommended.

A sample format is given in Table A4.6.

Table A4.6.   Sample format for manpower estimate

	Jan	Feb	Mar	Apr	May	Jun	Jul	Aug	Sep	Oct	Nov	Dec
Working days Fred Mary												

A4.6.3 Costs

Are there any other costs your reviewers should know about?

A4.6.4 Skill deficiencies

Identify skill deficiencies which, if not remedied, will prevent you from carrying out your plan. List them with plans (and dates) for resolving the shortfall, and indicate who is responsible for making each plan happen. Table A4.7 may be useful here.

Table A4.7.   Skill deficiencies

Skill/education required	By when	Who

A4.6.5 New tools required for successful assessment

What new tools are required? By when must they be available? What is your suggested plan for obtaining them?

A4.6.6 Hardware and software

Do you need any extra hardware or software to perform the planned assessment?

A4.6.7 Regular data information

What data do you need from the development process which you are not receiving already, and what steps will you take to acquire it?

A4.7   Completion criteria

A4.7.1 Development

What are the risk exit criteria for development to exit the phase to which this plan pertains? Say what particular things will cause you to say 'stop' at the next checkpoint. Also, list any intermediate criteria.

A4.7.2 Risk assessment

What do *you* have to do to exit this stage? How will you know you have completed what was planned?

A4.7.3 Success

Describe how success of the plan will be measured. Possibilities might be:

- Delivery of a quality product on time (measure it?!)
- Your support at the next checkpoint on time
- Percent of checkpoints exited on time
- Percentage of risk management deliverables on time
- Percentage of timely and accurate risk assessments
- How much did risk management cost you, and what do you think it saved the project overall? (Hard to prove and contentious)
- Value-added by risk assessors as assessed by product manager
- Percentage of risks discovered late which have been subject to causal analysis and process improvement.

A4.7.4 Strategy for successive phases

Outline your strategy for successive phases of the assessment.

A4.7.5 Process improvement

Indicate how you will improve your own practice and pass on risk management experience gained on this project. This must at least include your plan to produce an experience report.

Appendix 5
Sample programming objectives

General objectives

1 Name the programming system of which the support will be part and where this offering fits into its structure.
2 Name the equipment for which the support is specifically intended.
3 Summarize the user requirements and information needs (as opposed to the objectives).
4 Summarize the intended programming interfaces for customers.
5 Summarize the RAS (Reliability, availability, and serviceability) characteristics which are detailed in later sections.
6 Summarize the most significant usability characteristics of the program.
7 If your proposed customers are already using some other system, computer or manual, for doing this work, how they will migrate to your system.
8 Include pointers to other references where the further detail is kept.

User requirements

Summarize the requirements, and point the reader to the source. Describe in detail the classes and characteristics of the end users of the product, the tasks they perform, and a description of the environment in which the proposed product will be used. Areas to be addressed include the following.

User classes

A user class is any group of people that interface with the product in a common way. User classes include: end users, operators, programmers, installers, etc. Not all classes will be the same for each product. The proportion of the total user population each user class constitutes should be identified.

User characteristics

These should be defined for at least the average user and the lowest level user, and be in sufficient detail to allow assessment of the usability requirements the product must meet. These characteristics are physical and cognitive:

- *Physical characteristics*   These cover such things as: ranges of body sizes; age and sex distribution; visual, auditory or human performance limitations; and other appropriate factors to be considered when designing a particular product for a particular class(es) of user(s).
- *Cognitive characteristics*   These cover abilities and acquired skills and knowledge such as: education level, typing skills, data processing knowledge, application knowledge, product knowledge, programming ability, etc. This also includes consideration of any training/education required for employment in the jobs users are performing. Identify the need for any self-instruction, prompting, error checking, or other user aids required. The extent to which users will be motivated to use the products should also be identified.

User environment

The user requirements should also contain relevant details about the environment in which the product will be used. These should cover:

- Physical environment factors such as general environment (e.g., supermarket, law office).
- Social environment factors such as ergonomic standards (e.g., DIN and other standards), legal constraints, employee relations, and career structure.
- Work environment factors such as stand-alone applications, host control, remote terminal operation, other products in the user's work location, etc. Any constraints on the amount and kind of work a user can do should also be defined.

Major tasks

The major tasks the user is expected to accomplish when using the product should be described for each class of user. Note that these are tasks to be performed by the user during work, which do not necessarily correspond one for one with the functions of your system. Typical tasks include: running an application; producing a letter; editing text; creating a database; creating a file; entering data; performing retail transactions, etc. The frequency and importance of each task should be identified.

All ancillary tasks the user will be expected to perform should be defined. Examples are installation, problem determination, recovery, and customer setup.

The extent to which your support will be needed in order to perform these tasks should be identified.

Configuration specifications

Products

Describe the requirements for support of, or exclusion of support of, specific products, including modifications to them:

- CPUs
- Primary storage used by the support
- Primary storage used by the user through use of the support
- Channels
- Control units
- I/O devices
- Auxiliary storage used by the support
- Auxiliary storage used by the user through use of support
- Nongraphic consoles
- Graphic devices
- T/P devices

Programs

Describe the requirements for support of, or exclusion of support of specific programs:

- Control programs (types, sizes and application-oriented components)
- Other programs (types and sizes)

Performance

1 Performance information should be given for all programming systems. Batch performance should be expressed as execution times (absolute numbers or ratios of performance to currently available products), and space requirements. Response times for terminal-oriented transactions should be given for interactive programming support for given configurations, workloads and environments.
2 All performance statements should be such that they are verifiable by measurement, with the technology required for the measurement certain to be known at the time the support is complete.
3 Performance statements in objectives should be of a form which is meaningful to customers. All of these statements will concern performance in particular operating system and hardware environments.

4 The effect on performance in systems in which the support is optional and not used should be stated.

Dependencies

Describe, in detail, any dependencies you have on other product work which is outside your sphere of control:

1 Products (equipment)
2 Programs

Standards

Include a list of applicable industry or internal standards to which your product should adhere.

Programming quality and service considerations

Development and service measures

Estimate each of the following measures for the level of the product:

1 Lines of code (KLOC). The size of the source code, customarily shown as thousands (K) of lines of code (LOC) in two measures:
   (a) SSI (shipped source instruction)—the number of noncommentary source statements that make up the shipped product (including CSI).
   (b) CSI (changed source instructions)—the number of new and changed source statements.

   Also state whether the product and KLOC are add-on to, or replacement for, the preceding product level.
2 Pregeneral availability defects. Estimate the number of major defects to be detected during each inspection operation and each testing stage from unit test up to general availability. We described a way of doing this in Chapter 3.
3 Postgeneral availability defects. Estimate the number of valid defects you expect in the SSI and CSI KLOC (see 1), and state the assumptions for discovery of base defects. If more than one level of the product are current at any time, make separate statements about the numbers of defects you expect to have to migrate through earlier versions.

Implementation RAS factors

1 Implementation language: what programming language you will use.
2 Programming inspections: briefly describe the plans for defect discovery and

removal through high- and low-level design inspections, code inspections, and test plan and test case inspections.

Programming RAS characteristics

Make statements about the way you will build in the right amounts of RAS (reliability, availability, and serviceability). Describe the RAS design character- istics of the program, including RAS interactions with the system, other products, and components. Emphasis should be on product-level implications and design of RAS characteristics. Specific functional RAS characteristics should be described elsewhere.

Isolation/protection

Describe the measures taken to prevent destruction of code and data. Describe how interaction exposures are minimized with other components and users. List the system protection mechanisms used. Explain the techniques for physical and logical separation of code, control blocks, and buffers.

Termination/restart

Describe the restart capabilities after a catastrophic error. Specify the conditions for restart, restart causes, and effect on the system and users. Describe the termination activities required for restarting.

Dynamic update/migration

Describe the support that will permit dynamic product updates and migration for updating component code, changing component options, reconfiguration, re- lease, and system independence. List the restrictions that require a re-IPL or restart.

Distribution of program packages

Identify the packaging and structure of the program materials distribution:

- Source and object code
- Install packages

Usability objectives

These should address overall system usability in sufficient detail to understand clearly how the product should be designed, developed, and tested. Identify measurable usability criteria as a result of analysing user requirements and usability characteristics of comparable and competitive products. Areas to be addressed include the following.

Comparable/competitive usability data

Previous comparable products and competitive products should be measured and assessed and those data used to form the basis for the usability criteria described below.

Measurable usability criteria

Specific usability criteria for each task should be established for each user class. These criteria must be measurable and/or observable and should include, at least, the following for each major task:

- Amount of time to learn to do the task with the product
- Amount of time to do the task with the product (after learning)
- Percentage of users who must complete the task successfully
- Amount and kind of assistance (including the source)
- User's attitude about the usability of performing the task (use a scale of 1 to 5 where 1 is 'very satisfied')

Other criteria that may be appropriate are: performance and productivity-related measures such as response time, number and types of errors and throughput; measures against applicable ergonomic standards such as legibility and consistency of terminology and formats; and measures of overall satisfaction. Particular attention should be given to identifying to what extent existing knowledge and skills need to be unlearned in order to learn the new system or product.

Publications and terminology

Describe briefly what level of publications, online tuition or online help the customer needs. New or changed terminology has an impact on the user and should be kept to a minimum.

Multinational support

Some brief words about the level of multinational support intended if this is an international program.

Economic justification

Describe the business case for the units including the conditions which will affect the use and acceptance of the support. Include the target date for announcement and general availability and, if applicable, a range of prices that will satisfy a portion of the customer requirements. Original software developer (OSD) price and schedule objectives should also be addressed.

Representative competitive analysis

If this is programming support for new or unique significant devices or functions, or involves a significant development expenditure, then the following representative competitive analysis is required where adequate information is available:

1   Describe the differences, both advantages and deficiencies, between this programming support and (a reasonable number of) significant existing or planned competitive products. (Competition includes major manufacturers and computer programming development houses.)

    Differences in the following aspects of programming support should be included:
  (a)   Function
  (b)   Performance
  (c)   Reliability, availability and serviceability (RAS)
  (d)   Usability
  (e)   Price
  (f)   Extendibility

2   Provide an assessment (better, equal, deficient) of the programming support versus each comparable and competitive product, and give supporting reasons.

This can be followed by individual objectives for each of the individual functions which the product will contain.

Appendix 6
Individual function objectives

To accompany the overall objectives description for the product, there needs to be an individual description for each function, line item, or testable unit.

Brief description

A brief description of the function provided by this item, corrections or changes to the existing system design, or any other reason why the item has been included. Include the description of the problem and a management synopsis of the solution.

Justification

Describe why the change or addition is required and the origin of the requirement. Do not include any information relative to the solution or how it solves the problem.

Objectives

Describe what criteria should be used to judge the design, in terms of required function, performance, usability, and any other factors, such as cost.

Requirements

Describe what is needed from the user's point of view. Do not repeat what you have said elsewhere. If you have a requirements database, merely point at the IDs of requirements which this objective will address.

Existing support and deficiencies

Briefly describe what support, if any, your product currently provides, and tell why it is inadequate. This is a statement of the problem. See also 'justification'.

Background

This section is optional and can be omitted if necessary. Mention any relevant information about the history of this item, for example, why it was considered but rejected in a previous release.

Objective

The objective describes what must be provided to address the requirements. Try to write in the future tense: 'the function will . . .'.

User classes

List the classes of users of this line item (full descriptions will be in the introductory section).

Function provided

Describe at an abstract level any specific functions which must be addressed by the specifications in order to satisfy the requirements.

User tasks

Describe each of the tasks that users of this line item might want to perform, and relate this to the users listed in the previous section. State what the user is willing to do to accomplish each task, and also state what the user is not willing to do, i.e., it may be that the user is not required to do anything new to use this item.

This description will probably be at a level lower than the description in the introduction.

Migration/co-existence objectives

Make a positive statement regarding compatibility with previous versions and releases. Describe any special compatibility requirements. Specifically mention any incompatibilities that are to be permitted.

The remaining sections are all optional. These sections should be used only if the line item has more specific requirements that go beyond those mentioned that are applicable to the entire product. You are advised to ensure that sections are marked 'N/A' if they have been considered but not used.

Specific configuration objectives

Describe the support requirements for specific other products, both hardware and software, if any. (The section 'configuration specifications' in Appendix 5 lists all of the hardware products that will be supported by this release. However, if this item is meant to support a specific new device, it should be mentioned here.)

Specific performance objectives

Describe any specific performance objectives that are required of this item, if any.

Specific dependency objectives

Describe what external dependencies are, or are not, acceptable for this item. Dependencies are those things which are required or used by this item, but are beyond the control of your organization. For example, does this item require cooperation from another program, availability of certain hardware, etc?

Specific standards objectives

Describe any special requirements for this item that relate to company or external standards.

Specific usability objectives

Describe any specific usability objectives for this item. Identify and list the measurable usability criteria, if any. These include:

- Amount of time to learn to do the task with the product
- Amount of time to do the task with the product
- Percentage of users who must complete the task successfully
- Amount and kind of assistance they will need
- User's attitude about the usability of performing the task

Other criteria that may be appropriate are: performance and productivity related measures such as response time, number and types of errors, etc.

Specific publications and terminology objectives

Describe any special objectives for this item.

Specific international objectives

Describe any special requirements that relate to the use of this item in specific countries, including specifically any requirements which relate to non-English languages or special national-use character sets.

Appendix 7
Sample document of understanding

A document of understanding (DOU) is a way of ensuring that risks which you can identify, but which are outside your sphere of management control, are addressed. The DOU is an agreement between you and the other management group about things that will pass between your organizations during your development project. The document should be agreed between two DOU coordinators, one from each organization, although a responsible person should be identified for each deliverable passing between the organizations, and the commitment of that person to what the DOU says should be obtained by the coordinator. Depending on the type of agreement, some of the considerations for inclusion are:

- A clear and concise statement of what the end result of the agreement will be, for example, the delivery of a joint product set to the specified function and quality on a given date (an objective for the DOU).
- A description of every item or piece of information which is to pass between the two parties, with an agreed quality level, a date, a deliverer, and a receiver.
- Agreement with respect to all aspects of funding, pricing, or other financial matters.
- Assignment or transfer of manpower: how many, for how long, type of skills required or agreement on a by-name basis.
- The period to be covered by the agreement, start date to completion date.
- Plan of action to be followed. What progress reviews and reports are required? When and to whom are they submitted?
- Penalties, if any, for failure to meet commitments and schedules.
- Schedule dates for completion of key tasks, i.e., product developed, tested, etc.
- Clearly identified channels of communications.
- Responsibilities of each organization on matters such as forecast assumptions, product objectives and specifications, contact with outside suppliers, and cost estimates.

- How will success on the part of the performing organization be determined?
- Designation of names of key responsible individuals in each organization.
- If any responsibilities transfer, establish agreed-upon date(s) for transfer and outline how it will be accomplished.
- Agreement of other parties who must participate.
- Definition of terms.
- Ensure that you are clear how all the items agreed in the DOU will be tracked, and if possible how you will get advance warning of late running at the related site through their own risk assessment process.
- Ensure that you have a properly controlled mechanism for making changes to the DOU.

And a final watchword—with all plans, the norm should be that the reality happens according to plan. The emphasis with all status reporting must be that deviations from the plan are unacceptable; the response from the owner of the deviating item should be to report how the deviation is occurring, and the steps being taken to get back on target. Deviations from plans must be honestly reported, status reporting must occur at regular intervals, and any change to the plan must be tightly controlled. Tracking a DOU is harder than tracking a project. You cannot see the whites of their eyes when they give their report.

The three main failings of DOUs with which the authors have been involved have been:

- Failure to get them off the ground properly, to liaise with the right people, to get proper management agreement that there should be a DOU at all, or to get it signed off in time to be of practical use.
- Failure to get honest tracking information from the other party.
- Failure to agree and enforce function and quality standards for deliverables.

Appendix 8
Service-level agreements (SLAs)

In the 'market-driven quality' view of the world, several different attributes of your organization's business are examined, understood and possibly documented:

- Mission
- Customers
- Suppliers
- Objectives
- Strategy
- Process
- Dependencies
- Critical success factors
- Deliverables
- Procedures
- Management control
- Change control
- Process improvement

Two of these are worth examining under the heading of 'risks outside your span of control'.

First, who are your suppliers? Who delivers things to you? Simple things like furniture, computer equipment, etc. Second, having identified all the people whom you realize do things for you, there is another bunch of more nebulous items under the heading 'critical success factors'—these are things you actually depend on to do your job, but may well not realize because you take them for granted. If they were ever taken away, your project would sink. An example of this is your mainframe computer service, run by another department, outside your span of control.

While it is not worth setting up a full DOU with these groups, you could undertake a 'service-level agreement', so that you are clear from the start what they will provide for you during development, how you will measure it, and what you will do if it fails to meet expectations.

Further reading

This is a representative list of reading material that can be used to provide more background information and support, mainly for the topics introduced in Chapter 5 onwards.

Baker, A. L., Bieman, J. M., Fenton, N., Gustafson, D. A., Melton, A. and Whitty, R. (1990). 'A philosophy for software measurement', *J. Systems Software*, vol. 12, pp. 277–81.

Boehm, B. W. (1988). 'A spiral model of software development and enhancement', *Computer*, May 1988, 61–72. Reprinted in *Software Risk Management*, Boehm, B. W. (ed.), IEEE Computer Society Press, Washington DC, 1989.

Brooks, F. P. Jr. (1986). 'No silver bullet: essence and accidents of software engineering' in *Information Processing '86*, Kugler, H.-J. (ed.), Elsevier, North-Holland.

Coward, P. D. (1990). 'Software testing techniques' in *The Software Life Cycle*, Andrews, D. and Ince, D. (eds), Butterworth, Oxford.

Currit, P. A., Dyer, M. and Mills, H. D. (1986). 'Certifying the reliability of software', *IEEE Trans. Software Engineering*, vol. SE-12, no. 1, pp. 3–11.

Defense Systems Management College (1983). 'Risk assessment techniques' in *DSMC Handbook*, Ch. 4 and Appendix F, July 1983, pp. F-1 to F-13). Reprinted in *Software Risk Management*, Boehm, B. W. (ed.), IEEE Computer Society Press, Washington DC, 1989.

Fagan, M. E. (1986). 'Advances in software inspections', *IEEE Trans. Software Engineering*, vol. SE-12, no. 7, pp. 744–51.

Gilb, T. (1988). *Principles of Software Engineering Management*, Addison-Wesley, Wokingham. (Especially Ch. 6 'Estimating the risk; and Ch. 12 'The inspection process: early quality and process control'.)

Green, S., Kouchakdjian, A., Basili, V. R. and Weidow, D. (1990). 'The cleanroom case study in the software engineering laboratory: project description and early analysis', *NASA Software Engineering Laboratory Series*, SEL-90-02, Goddard Space Flight Center, Greenbelt, Maryland.

Hauser, J. R. and Clausing, D. (1988). 'The house of quality', *Harvard Business Review*, May–June, pp. 63–73.

Humphrey, W. S. (1989). *Managing the Software Process*, Addison-Wesley, Wokingham. (Especially Ch. 17 'Defect prevention'.)

Humphrey, W. S. (1991). 'Characterizing the software process: a maturity framework', *Technical Report*, CMU/SEI-87-TR-11, Software Engineering Institute, Carnegie-

Mellon University, Pittsburgh. Also Paulk, M. C., Curtis, B. and Chrissis, M. B. (1991). 'Capability maturity model for software', CMU/SEI-91-TR-24.

Kan, S. H. (1991). 'Modelling and software development quality', *IBM Systems Journal*, vol. 30, no. 3, pp. 351–62.

King, R. (1989). *Better Designs in Half the Time: Implementing Quality Function Deployment in America*, 3rd edn,. GOAL/QPC, Methuen, MA.

Praxis (on behalf of the United Kingdom Department of Trade and Industry) (1992). *Quantum: A Measurement-Based Framework for the Assurance of Software Quality*, HMSO.

Selby, R. W., Basili, V. R. and Baker, F. T. (1987). 'Cleanroom software development: an empirical evaluation', *IEEE Trans. Software Engineering*, vol. SE-13, no. 9, pp. 1027–37.

Shepperd, M. (1990). 'An evaluation of software product metrics' in *The Software Life Cycle*, Andrews, D. and Ince, D. (eds), Butterworth, Oxford.

Whitgift, D. (1991). *Methods and Tools for Software Configuration Management*, John Wiley, Chichester.

Index